The ULTIMATE book of KITCHEN HINTS

LESLEY WICKHAM

BayBooks
An imprint of HarperCollinsPublishers

A Bay Books Publication

Bay Books, an imprint of
HarperCollins *Publishers* Pty Ltd
25 Ryde Road, Pymble, Sydney NSW 2073, Australia
31 View Road, Glenfield, Auckland 10, New Zealand

Text Copyright © Lesley Wickham 1987
Revised Edition 1993

National Library of Australia
Cataloguing-in-Publication data:
Wickham, Lesley
The Ultimate Book of Kitchen Hints
Rev. ed.
ISBN 1 86378 133 1

1. Cookery — Miscellaneous I. Title
641.5
Printed in Singapore
Illustrations Gerry Murphy

9 8 7 6 5 4 3 2
96 95 94 93

CONTENTS

LOOKING AFTER YOUR KITCHEN

STALE CIGARETTE SMELLS

If you are a non-smoker and have friends who smoke, you may well dislike the smell of cigarettes, which can linger for some time in a room after your guests have left.

To remove the smell, put an open dish of water in the room and fill all emptied ashtrays with water while they are waiting to be washed up. This dispels the odours after a little while. After an evening party, place one or two bowls of water in the room and leave all the emptied ashtrays filled with water overnight. In the morning, the smell will have faded considerably.

WASHING UP STICKY DISHES

Dishes or utensils which have been used for sticky food can be difficult to wash up. As a rule, wash foods with a high proportion of fat or sugar (such as buttercream or honey) in warm water as this will melt the food. Wash foods with flour or eggs in cold water because hot water cooks the mixture onto the utensil making it even harder to remove. When in doubt, cold is safer.

FLOORS

CHOOSING A FLOORING MATERIAL

Kitchen floors constantly collect food scraps, splashes and cooking spatters. These not only become smelly after a while but can also be a source of disease. Add to this the problem of scraps of food being tracked out of the kitchen and across other floors on people's feet and you have good cause to want to keep them clean.

Ideally, kitchen floors should be of a non-absorbent material so that they can be washed thoroughly. Kitchen carpets might be tempting in the shop but they can be difficult to clean in practice. Tiles and sheet floorings are generally more practical for a busy family.

The floor should not be so smooth that it will be slippery when wet, as this can lead to falls — a danger particularly when you happen to be carrying a hot, heavy pan of food! At the same time, it should not be so rough or textured that food lodging in the crevices will be difficult to remove. Tiles may offer a wider variety of textures than sheet flooring and they provide a cooler surface in a hot climate.

However, if you have clumsy people around, or perhaps small children, learning to help in the kitchen, it might be wise to choose a softer surface, like cork or sheet vinyl or lino, so that china or glasses dropped will bounce rather than break. These floors generally do not feel as cold as tiles.

CLEANING THE FLOOR

Scuffmarks

Dark scuff marks on the floor can sometimes be removed with an ordinary ink rubber (you can usually find one by raiding the children's school bag if you haven't one handy). These marks are often caused by the black rubber feet on the bottoms of furniture legs. They can be avoided by replacing these feet with lighter-coloured or non-rubber feet.

Terrazzo

Many proprietary cleaning products make concrete or terrazzo floors slippery in order to give them a shine. You can make your own inexpensive polish by mixing equal parts of vinegar and household kerosene. Apply it with a mop and the floor will come up clean and shiny without being slippery.

Cork floors

These normally only need mopping over with a moist (but not too wet) mop or floor sponge for a sparkling finish. Loose dirt can be swept or vacuumed off the surface. A plastic scourer will take off trodden-in food without damaging the surface. For really stubborn marks, try fine steel wool with a little turpentine. This actually removes some of the surface glaze and takes the stain with it. Wax the floor afterwards to seal it again, or apply a coat of cork sealer.

THE KITCHEN SINK

CLEANING CHROME TAPS

Clean around chrome taps with a toothbrush to remove that grease build-up which accumulates there. Polish them with methylated spirits or metal cleaner for a beautiful shine.

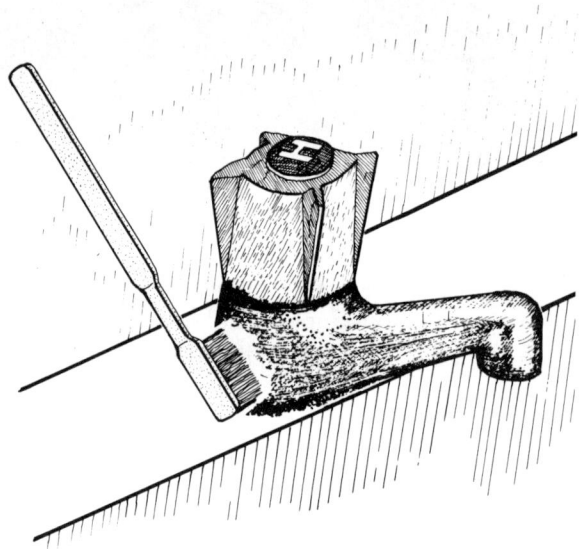

AVOID BLOCKAGES IN THE KITCHEN SINK

The best treatment for a blocked kitchen sink is prevention! Your sink will not become blocked if you are always careful that you DO NOT:

• put tea leaves down the sink (they accumulate and clog the S-bend). Put these on the garden or on your pot plants.

• put dry materials which are likely to swell up down the sink — semolina, flour, rice, gelatine, pastry scraps. Put these in the garbage bin. If necessary, brush them into a plastic bag first to keep them confined.

• pour hot fats down the sink (they can congeal and set in the pipes). Allow these to cool and solidify and then put them in the garbage bin.

CURE BLOCKAGES IN THE KITCHEN SINK

The remedy for a blocked sink depends very much on the cause. You won't always know the cause, so you will have to take a punt and try the remedies below in the order they are presented. If, however, you have a fair idea that you have been putting a particular something down there which you shouldn't have (see previous page), you may be in a better position to choose the right approach.

If a sink is blocked with congealed grease, the solution lies in melting it so it can be flushed away. Try pouring boiling water directly into the plug hole. If this doesn't work, or if the sink already contains a lot of water, you may need to push a piece of wire down the pipe to try to make a hole in the plug of fat, so that some of the water can get through the blockage. When the water is able to drain out slowly, pour boiling water after it to melt away the rest of the fat. This may take some time and may require alternately poking down the wire and pouring in the hot water.

If the blockage is very bad, you may need to pour a solution of caustic soda (use about a tablespoon to half a bucket of water) down the sink. This will usually dissolve the grease and allow it to run away. Be careful handling the caustic solution as it can burn your skin.

If the sink is blocked with solid matter, neither of these methods is likely to work and it will probably need clearing in a more physical way. A simple suction cup on a stick (available from hardware stores) pumped vigorously over the drain hole can loosen the blockage and allow it to wash away. Failing this, you will need to put a large bucket under the S-bend and undo the locking nut on the pipe. This will open the pipe and you can then clear away the blockage by hand. Be sure to fasten the nut tightly again and test it before removing the bucket!

RE-USE STEEL WOOL

Steel wool won't go rusty if it is kept from contact with the air. Keep a screwtop jar filled with soapy water in your cleaning cupboard and return the steel wool to it each time it is used. If the steel wool is covered with the water, it will not rust.

SHINE LAMINATED SURFACES

After cleaning your laminated bench top, you can bring up a lovely shine by polishing it with a soft cloth dipped in methylated spirits.

RUBBER GLOVES IN HOT WEATHER

Rubber gloves can be unpleasant in hot weather as they can cause the hands to sweat most uncomfortably. Prevent this by wearing a thin pair of cotton gloves inside them. These will absorb the perspiration and make the work more comfortable.

SMELLY GARBAGE BINS

Garbage bins in the kitchen can be protected by lining them with bin liners or old supermarket carrier bags. This will make it easier to remove the garbage and the bin needs only a light rinse out from time to time.

However, with the best of care, they can sometimes become smelly. Rinse them out with a weak bleach solution and stand them in the sun. Alternatively, if they are very bad, stand a dish containing a mixture of equal parts of vinegar and Condy's crystals in the bin (outside, preferably). This will neutralise the smell.

ANTS IN THE KITCHEN

Ants can be a problem in the kitchen, especially after rain. If they have found something they like and made a trail in your kitchen, you can deter them by wiping a cut lemon over the trail or even by wiping over an area of the trail with the dishcloth, when it is still hot and soapy after washing up.

Deter them from coming in by leaving a small dish of borax and sugar near their entry point. Warning: borax is toxic so keep it away from pets and children. If ants are a real problem, they should be cleared by a licensed pest exterminator.

PROTECT RECIPE BOOKS

Good recipe books are an investment and it is a great pity when they become spattered with food while you are cooking. This can be prevented by using a clear, perspex cookery book stand, which props the book up, open at the right page, and protects it from splashes.

An inexpensive alternative is to put your cookery book, open at the page, into a plastic bag and prop it up on the bench. Splashes can be wiped away or, if necessary, thrown away with the bag.

SCREWTOP LIDS THAT STICK

If you can't get the lid off a screwtop jar, run the lid (not the rest of the jar) under the hot tap for a minute or two. This expands the lid more than the jar and it will usually come off. A light tap with a knife handle or scissors might help.

CAN OPENERS RUN BETTER

Does your can opener tend to stick or be stiff? Try immersing it in hot water for a few minutes before you use it.

CANDLES FOR ROMANCE

Have you ever bought candles for a special dinner only to find that the bottoms would not fit into your special candlesticks? Have you spent messy and frustrating time trying to shave enough off them to push them in? You can solve this problem quickly and easily by dipping the ends into boiling water for a minute or two to soften them and then immediately pushing them firmly into the candlestick.

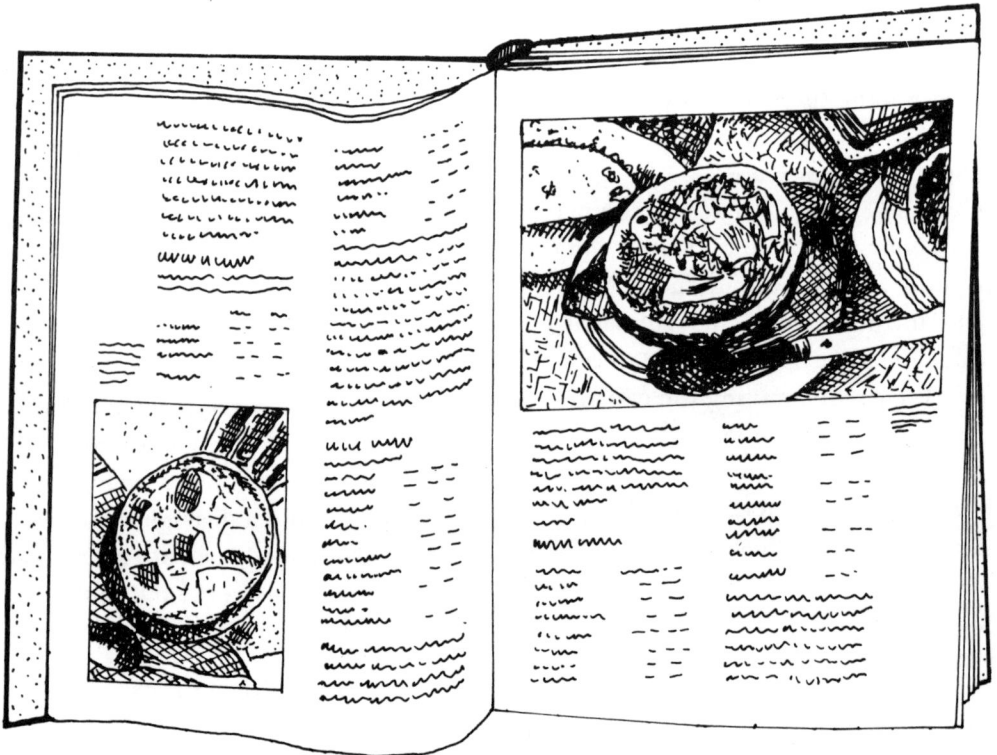

The excess should push up out of the way. If the difference is too great, squeeze the candle ends thinner with your fingers while they are hot from the water. They should then fit.

If you have the opposite problem and the candlesticks are too big for the candles, tear off a little strip of aluminium foil and wrap it around the bottom, just high enough to reach the top of the socket in the candlestick. Use as many layers as necessary to fit your holder. The candle will stand there firmly and no-one will be any the wiser.

Candles which drip wax excessively can be restrained (to a degree) by leaving them in the refrigerator all day before they are to be used. The wax cools and tends to set the drips on the way down before they reach the table. (In very hot weather, this effect may not last long!)

FRESH-SMELLING CHOPPING BOARDS

Although there are many types of plastic boards available today, many cooks still prefer wooden chopping boards because of their kindness to good knives and their aesthetic quality. They do, unfortunately, have a tendency to absorb smells from strong foods like onion and garlic.

If your board becomes smelly after preparing a strong food, rinse it thoroughly with a weak bleach solution or, if it is really bad, leave it to soak in the solution in the sink for 5–10 minutes. Rinse off the bleach with clean water. Any residual bleach smell will disappear as the board dries, leaving the wood fresh again.

PREVENT WOODEN CHOPPING BOARDS DRYING OUT

Wooden chopping boards are less likely to absorb smells and will last longer if the wood is conditioned from time to time with oil. If you find that the colour of the wood is rather faded, pour a few drops of cooking oil onto the surface and gently rub it in all over with a piece of paper towel. Add more if necessary, to give a good coating, cleaning off the excess with the paper towel. Leave it overnight, and in the morning rinse it well with clean warm water. This will keep the wood conditioned and reduce its tendency to split and to absorb smells.

CLEANING FOOD FROM DIFFICULT EQUIPMENT

Crumbs in the toaster

Like any other electrical appliance, toasters must not be washed in water and should never be cleaned or unjammed while they are still connected to the power outlet.

Sharp instruments should not be used near the elements as this could damage them. Use a pastry brush or a soft toothbrush to clean crumbs away from inaccessible parts. Don't shake or hit the toaster to remove crumbs — this can damage the element.

As on the stove, any food or drink spills should be cleaned off the surface before the toaster is used again to prevent them burning. If any liquid is spilled into the elements, disconnect the toaster and make sure it is thoroughly dry before reconnecting it to the power.

Cleaning lemon rind from graters

Lemon rind (zest) is so good in so many foods but it can be very difficult to remove from the little grater holes. To remove most of the zest, run a straight-bladed knife across the surface of the grater. Then remove the remainder of the rind with a toothbrush.

Cleaning garlic from crushers

If your nightmare is getting the last bits of garlic out of the crusher, try pushing a fine metal skewer into the holes, or use a toothbrush, from the outside.

COOKER CARE

FOIL ON GRILL PANS STOPS THE DIRT
You can prevent food from burning onto the grill pan or the drip trays on your stove top by lining them with aluminium foil. This can be removed and thrown away when it is dirty, and replaced with a clean piece.

TOOTHBRUSH FOR CLEANING
There are always those difficult-to-reach parts of the stove and sink, such as around the taps, where a brown coat of fatty residue builds up. This can defy all attempts to clean it out. To remove residue, try scraping it with the point of a kitchen knife. Prevent it forming again by cleaning the area from time to time with a toothbrush dipped in cleaning liquid.

KEEPING THE STOVE CLEAN
When food burns onto your cooktop, avoid using harsh abrasives or scourers to remove it as this will damage the surface and make it more likely to stain the next time. Try a solution of ammonia, left on for a few hours or overnight and wiped off with plenty of hot water next day.

FISHY SMELLS IN COOKING PANS
Fish is very good cooked in the oven but it has a tendency to leave its smell behind in the dish from time to time.

To remove this smell put used tea leaves out of the pot (or several used tea bags) into the dish and fill it up with water. Leave it standing for 15–30 minutes and then rinse it out thoroughly. The smell should be gone.

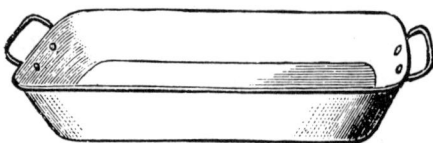

REFRIGERATORS AND FREEZERS

POLISH THE REFRIGERATOR
To give your refrigerator and freezer a beautiful shine which will resist dirtying, polish it with car polish. It will only need this once or twice a year and marks will sponge off the surface more easily.

FRESHER REFRIGERATORS
A refrigerator is, for the most part, a closed space, and is very prone to collect smells which can spread easily between foods and spoil their flavour. There are several ways to reduce this problem:
• Defrost and clean out the refrigerator regularly, as the frost layer can absorb smells and recycle them to other foods. If you have a frost-free refrigerator, clean it out regularly to remove any accumulation of food scraps. These go off after a while and can make the refrigerator smell stale.
• Use a solution of bicarbonate of soda (about a teaspoon to a bowl) instead of detergent to clean the refrigerator. Detergent leaves a smell which can get into the food.
• Always rinse the refrigerator with water after cleaning it. If it has an unpleasant smell, pour a few drops of vanilla essence or lemon juice into the water. This will make it smell fresher.
• Always cover foods in the refrigerator. Some foods contaminate others with their smell, while liquids or very moist foods left uncovered are apt to increase the frost build-up. This wastes power and the refrigerator will need defrosting more often.
• Make sure foods are quite cold when they go into the refrigerator. Otherwise they will produce steam as they cool and frost up the refrigerator.

• Never leave the refrigerator door open — this raises the temperature. Not only can it spoil the contents, but it also adds unnecessary frost build-up while everything cools down again.

ICE CUBES

To prevent ice-cube trays sticking to the freezer shelf, smear the undersides with glycerine.

Ice cubes in a frost-free freezer will gradually evaporate if left in their tray. This is because the freezer stays frost free by constantly exhausting moist air to the outside.

You can prevent ice cubes drying out by storing them in a canister with a lid inside the freezer. This makes them easier to get out when needed.

The same applies to any liquids stored in the freezer. If not covered, they will constantly become more dehydrated and hence more concentrated.

GLASS CARE

GLASSES STUCK TOGETHER

Glasses should not be stored inside each other as they have a tendency to stick. It is easy to break one while trying to get it out.

If they do stick, fill the inside one with iced water to make it contract. Then stand the outside one in warm (not hot) water in the sink or in a bowl. You should be able to pull them apart after a minute or so.

PROTECT FINE GLASSES IN WASHING

Fine glasses are easily broken as they knock against the hard surface of the sink. For especially precious glasses, line the sink with an old towel before washing them. This provides a cushion to prevent them breaking.

HOLLOW-STEMMED GLASSES

Do the hollow stems of your best glasses give you nightmares to clean? Use a pipe cleaner or a cotton bud to clean out any film or debris and then rinse them under hot running water. Drain them upside-down on a rack until completely dry.

STAINED GLASS VASES

Glass vases sometimes collect a build-up of dead vegetable matter in the bottom which can spoil the appearance of the vase. This can be removed by putting some sand in the vase and covering it to the level of the top of the stain with warm water containing washing-up detergent. Leave the vase to stand for a few hours, giving it a good swish around each time you walk past. If necessary, use an old spoon or dish mop to rub it around once or twice. The sandy water can be tipped out later, leaving a clean surface.

REMOVING MILK FILM ON GLASSES

The best way to avoid this problem is to train your family to rinse out milk glasses with COLD water as soon as they finish with them. Failing this, rinse them in cold water before washing them. Putting them into hot water cooks the milk solids onto the surface and makes them harder to clean.

TEMPERING GLASSES AND JARS

Glassware which is subjected to sudden changes of temperature (glasses used for hot drinks or jars used for preserving or jam making) can be tempered to make it more resistant to the cracking caused by these temperature changes.

Put the glasses in a saucepan taller than the tallest glass item and cover them with cold water. Bring them slowly to the boil and continue boiling for an hour, without letting the water level fall below the top of the glass. Cool them slowly in the water before removing them.

LEAKY CORKS IN BOTTLES

Corks in bottles are, for the most part, very good seals to keep out the air and preserve the contents. However, if they leak they are likely to make a mess as the contents get out, and the contents will go off as the air gets in. To prevent this, regularly check the corks of long-storage liquids and wines. If they are leaking, they will usually show signs of moisture or discolouration around the edges. Melt some candle wax (perhaps the tail end of a candle) with a little beeswax, lard or kerosene (to soften it and reduce cracking when it hardens). Push the cork in well and dip the top in the wax mixture. As it hardens, it will create an air-tight seal at the top of the cork.

then wipe the pan out with a piece of paper towel and some salt. Wipe the surface thoroughly and then put the pan away.

SAUCEPAN LIDS

Do saucepan lids fall out of your pan cupboard in all directions when you open the door? Do you have trouble finding the lid you want? Try making a lid rack for the inside of the door. Nail a bead of wood across to support the rim, then attach loops of elastic, shock cord or spiral plastic-covered cord measured to the width of each lid at half-a-lid's width above this. Thread the lids in and let them rest on the timber bead on their edge. The lids will always be handy when needed.

PAN PRESERVATION

CLEANING ALUMINIUM PANS

To prevent sauces and sticky food making the surface of your aluminium saucepans into a cleaning nightmare, fill each pan with warm water as soon as you serve the food and leave it to soak while you eat the meal. By the time you are ready to wash up, most food will simply rinse away.

PANCAKE AND OMELETTE PANS

The secret to successful pancakes and omelettes is a flat, shallow pan, preferably with a heavy base. The pan shouldn't be washed in detergent but only wiped over between uses, or rinsed in warm water. You can use the same pan for pancakes and omelettes as they will both benefit from this treatment. It will ensure that your pancakes and omelettes won't stick to the pan.

If the pan does become sticky, treat its surface by heating a little vegetable oil in it and swirling it around. Tip it out and

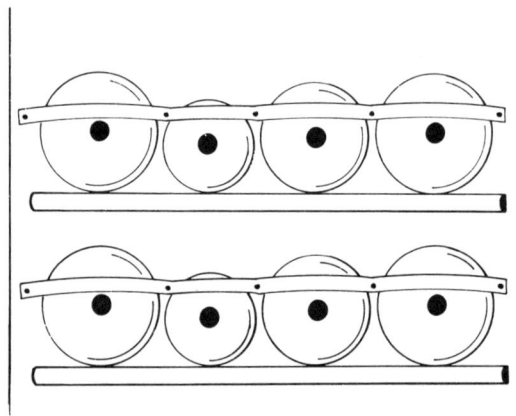

PRESSURE COOKERS

Pressure cookers are wonderful aids to a busy cook but the rings can be quite a problem to replace. The rubber seal will eventually perish no matter how careful you are, but you can slow down the process. As soon as you take off the lid, run cold water on the rubber ring to harden it. This will help it to resist damage from handling. If it is possible with the model you have, store the ring separately from the lid between uses.

RESTORE THE OLD KETTLE

Is your kettle furrier inside than the coat of your pet cat or dog? This is a build-up of alkaline minerals from the water. You can remove it by soaking it overnight with a solution of a safe food acid, like vinegar or lemon juice (about a tablespoon per half a litre of water). Rinse it out thoroughly the next day and then boil it with fresh water which should then be discarded. Repeat the treatment if necessary and the surface should gradually come clean.

KNIFE STORAGE

If steel knives (not stainless) have to be stored for any length of time, coat them lightly with vaseline and wrap them in cling wrap or greaseproof paper. This will prevent air and moisture getting to the blades and they will not rust.

SILVER, COPPER AND BRASS

SILVERWARE

Silverware becomes tarnished in contact with foods high in sulphur, such as eggs. A cheap and effective cleaning bath can be made using an old aluminium pan and washing soda. Put all the items you want to clean into the aluminium saucepan and add about 25 g washing soda per litre of water. Boil this up for a few minutes and then rinse the silverware thoroughly. It should be bright again. This method is very good for cleaning highly ornamented or fiddly pieces, even jewellery. Make sure the ventilation is good while you do this as it tends to have an unpleasant smell. (If the items will not fit into the pan, use another type of bowl and place an aluminium lid or pan in the hot water with the soda and the dirty items.)

Another way to clean egg stains from silver cutlery is to dip the cutlery into the water the eggs are boiling in.

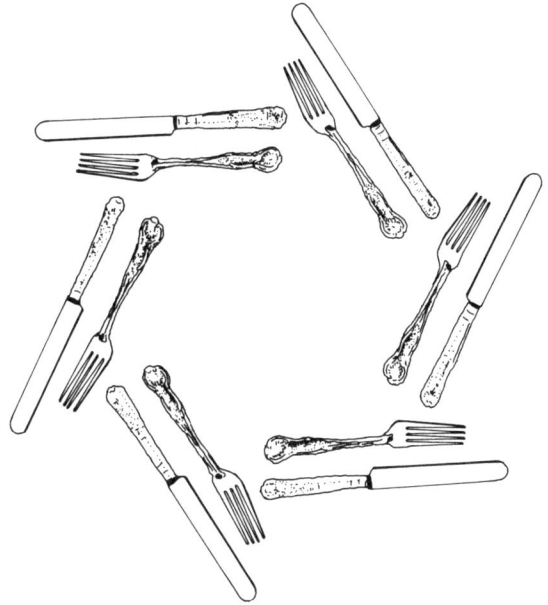

CLEANING SILVER PLATE

Thin silver plate is easily damaged by harsh cleaning, which rubs away the surface. One way to clean it without harm is to mix a tablespoon of borax (warning: this is toxic) and a little liquid soap with some hot water in a basin large enough to take the item to be cleaned. Top up with warm water and leave the article to soak for a few hours or overnight. Rinse it well and the tarnish should be removed completely.

STORING SILVERWARE

Silverware which isn't often used always seems to need cleaning when you get it out for a special occasion. You may end up not using it because you don't have time to clean it first.

To prevent silverware becoming tarnished, pack it in plastic bags when you have cleaned it. This will prevent it coming into contact with outside air and will slow down the tarnishing considerably.

COPPER CARE

If you have difficulty cleaning copper, try sprinkling some salt on half a lemon and rubbing it vigorously over the copper surface. Rinse the copper immediately in fresh water and it should be bright again, needing only a final polish to bring back a beautiful shine.

STAINS AND BURNS ON PANS AND EQUIPMENT

STAINLESS STEEL STAINS

Stainless steel should not, in the normal course of events, rust. However, this doesn't mean that it won't actually stain. Heat can discolour stainless steel pans, sinks and implements. To remove this discolouration, polish the area with fine steel wool dipped in lemon juice. The acid will clean the surface. Rinse the area and polish it if you wish with metal polish.

BURNT ALUMINIUM PANS

Most food stuck onto cooking pans will come off if you fill the pan with water and boil it up again for a few minutes. Let it cool to handling temperature and then wash up as usual. Badly-stuck food may need soaking overnight after boiling.

If you burn food onto a pan and can't remove it by soaking, try sprinkling the bottom of the pan with salt and then covering it with vinegar. Leave it to stand overnight and clean it out next day with a plastic scourer.

Alternatively, if you can stand the smell, soak a small towel in ammonia solution and then wrap the saucepan in it, pushing the ends of the towel inside the pan. Wrap the whole thing in a big plastic bag and leave it overnight. The burnt food should then clean off easily with a plastic scourer.

TEA AND COFFEE STAINS ON POTS AND CUPS

Cups and mugs with a shiny glaze are seldom susceptible to tea and coffee stains. However, earthy pottery with matt glazes may pick up a brown stain from the tannin in tea and coffee. To remove this, pour a teaspoon of bleach into the cup and fill it up with water. Leave it to stand overnight. In the morning, rinse it out. It should be quite clean. If you have a really stubborn patch, rub it with a plastic scourer during the rinse or even repeat the treatment with a slightly stronger bleach solution.

Alternatively, you can rub the stained area with salt, moistened with a little water. Rinse well afterwards. A badly-stained surface might need more than one application.

Tea and coffee pots can be cleaned in the same way as cups but really heavy build-ups might need several treatments.

Another solution is to mix a little washing soda in some hot water and leave this in the pot overnight. Clean the inside of the spout with a cotton bud dipped in the same solution. Rinse the pot out very thoroughly before using it.

A teapot spout can be very difficult to clean because of its shape and position. If it is not practical to immerse the pot entirely in a soaking solution, try packing the spout tightly with damp salt. Leave it overnight, and in the morning rinse it out with boiling water. The salt absorbs the stains and they rinse away with it. A very badly stained spout might need more than one application to clean it out completely.

MOISTURE RINGS ON WOODEN FURNITURE

If someone leaves a glass on your favourite table and it makes a milky ring, don't despair. Coat the area thickly with mayonnaise and leave it for a couple of hours. The stain should disappear.

HEAT STAINS ON WOODEN FURNITURE

A good table can easily be damaged by standing your favourite casserole on it without a mat underneath. Once there, stains are difficult to remove, but try this old remedy. Rub the stain thoroughly with kerosene, using a soft cloth. Then, with a clean cloth, rub in a little eau de cologne to remove the excess kerosene. (Try this on a hidden section of the table first, to make sure the treatment is compatible with the finish on the furniture!)

STAINS ON MARBLE OR ALABASTER

Marble and alabaster are used in many households as pastry slabs or ashtrays. These materials stain easily because they have a porous surface.

To clean stains from marble, rub a little lemon juice or vinegar into the surface with a soft cloth, then rinse well. Seal the surface, once it is clean, in the same way you would seal wooden boards, by polishing in a little cooking oil on a soft cloth. This fills the pores and prevents stains penetrating the surface.

Alabaster ashtrays can be cleaned this way, or by rubbing in a little turpentine. Again, rinse very well. Don't use this method on pastry boards as it can spoil the food.

VACUUM FLASKS

Vacuum flasks are best stored with the top slightly open. Part of the musty smell they tend to acquire can often be traced to moulds which have grown in any moisture left inside when they are sealed.

If they do become musty, the smell can be removed in two ways:
• Fill the flask with hot water and a teaspoon of bleach. Fasten the top on and leave it to stand for five minutes. Rinse out the flask with hot water. Allow to drain. The smell should be gone.
• Leave the flask to stand overnight filled with boiling water containing two teaspoons of bicarbonate of soda. Next day, rinse it out well.

WOODEN DISHES

Wooden bowls and dishes will keep better if they are not immersed in water. You can sponge out food residues with a moistened dishcloth but avoid using detergent. To keep these dishes at their best, gently rub the surface from time to time with a little vegetable oil. This seals and protects the wood and is safe to eat from. If a dish is badly marked, it can be sanded out gently in the direction of the grain with fine sandpaper and then thoroughly oiled again to seal the surface. (Several applications of oil might be needed to make a good seal.)

MANAGING MATTERS

LABELLING STORES

Always label bags or jars of food which you have packed yourself or which don't have a maker's label. At the time you pack them, you are sure you will always remember what the contents were. Months later, as you fish a packet of brown meat from the freezer or look at two jars of apparently identical buff-coloured powder to see which is wholewheat and which is rye flour, it is not so clear. Putting the date on the package, too, helps you see when a food might be too stale to use. Some foods age subtly (such as dried yeast) and it is not always obvious that they are no longer good.

MAKING A FORCING BAG

There is certainly a knack to using a forcing (icing) bag but, once you have mastered it, you can give a beautiful finish to all sorts of dishes. The best forcing bags are made of cloth, such as nylon, but you

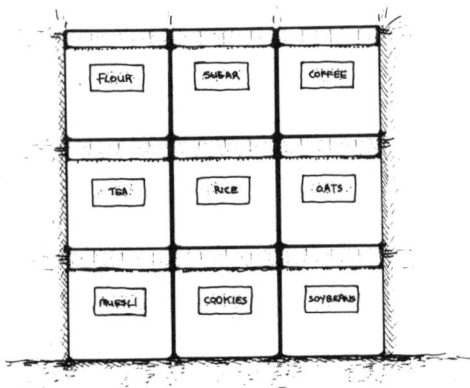

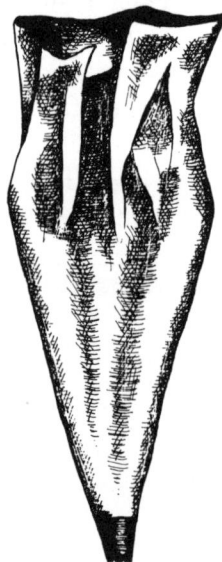

can make one with several layers of greaseproof paper if necessary. Simply cut a large rectangle, fold it in half to make a smaller one twice as thick, then roll it up into a cone shape. Pinch off a small piece of the tip, just large enough for the open part of the nozzle to come through. Too large a hole can allow the whole nozzle to escape, followed by the contents, as you squeeze out the mixture. Fold the corner which sticks out at the top down over the outside of the bag. This neatens the job and provides some reinforcement.

USING A FORCING BAG

Many a new cook is put off using forcing bags by a disastrous first experience of cream, potato, icing or meringue, or some other gooey mixture generously coating itself on the outside of the bag while filling and then refusing to come out at the right end.

The trick for clean filling is to hold the bag close to the nozzle and fold the upper part of the bag down over your hand. Holding your hand in a cone shape to keep the bag open, fill the bottom part, then roll the folded-over portion a little further up the bag until about half the bag is full. Don't try to put too much in at once. Now unfold the top part and pull the edges together. Twist them around once to seal in the contents and fold the excess fabric down the side of the full bag, closing the top tightly.

Hold your hand over the top of the bag and start to squeeze towards the nozzle. The pressure of your hand should be over the twisted top of the bag, preventing the contents from pushing out of the top again.

If you are using icing or something which tends to ooze slippery syrup through the fabric of the bag, you may need a bowl of water and a sponge to rinse your hand and to wipe the outside of the bag from time to time.

COOKING SMALL AMOUNTS

If you want to keep your vegetables separate and save on washing up at the same time, cook them in the same container but in separate parcels:

• By microwave: put each type of vegetable in a separate plastic bag, loosely tied at the top, and microwave them together, arranged with the hardest type (needing the longest cooking) toward the outside and the softest toward the centre.
• By heat: wrap them in separate parcels of foil and simmer them together in one saucepan. If they require different cooking times, you can drop shorter-cooking parcels into the pan after the longer-cooking parcels have been in for a suitable time.

COVERING CASSEROLES IF YOU DON'T HAVE A LID

If your recipe calls for a dish to be covered during the cooking and you don't have a suitable dish with a lid, you can improvise.

If you are cooking in the oven or on top of the stove, use aluminium foil to cover the pot. You can often get a better seal with this than with a lid, as the foil can be smoothed carefully down around the rim of the pot.

If you are cooking in a microwave, use plastic cling wrap, or turn a glass or china plate (without metal decoration, as this is not safe in the microwave) upside down over the cooking pot.

CLAYTONS DOUBLE BOILER

Unless you are keen and cook regularly, you probably don't think it worthwhile to have every piece of cooking equipment in

your kitchen. It is not only expensive — it has to be stored away when not in use. Not many sauces are made with eggs these days, but that doesn't mean that you might not want to use them occasionally, so should you buy a double boiler for that occasion? It can be very frustrating to find that special recipe and look around the kitchen for the double boiler you know you don't have.

A simple improvisation can deliver the same result. Choose your best non-stick small saucepan and find a large metal or enamel bowl or another saucepan into which the small one will fit snugly, leaving a small space all around and underneath it. Pour some water into the larger bowl or pan and sit the smaller one in it. Adjust the water level until it comes about half-way up the sides of the small saucepan and, hey presto, you have a double boiler.

USING THE MICROWAVE

THE EXPLODING FOOD SYNDROME

There are times when you wish you had never heard of a microwave oven, especially when some food has just

exploded in it. The problem is that the soft interior of things like egg yolks or whole eggs, pumpkins, tomatoes, apples and so on, gets hot faster than the skin. As it gets hot, the interior has to expand and, with a skin in the way, it has nowhere to go. Eventually, the pressure builds up to a level where the skin gives way and suddenly you have food splattered all over the inside of your oven.

The simple answer to this problem is to prick, cut or remove the skins or shells of foods before they go in the microwave. This allows an escape route for the steam and the food will stay where it belongs.

MORE EVEN COOKING IN YOUR MICROWAVE

Have you ever found that your microwaved cake is still raw at the bottom (especially in the middle) when it seemed to be cooked on the top or even overdone? This is particularly common with microwave convection ovens and there is a simple explanation and solution for it.

Microwave ovens cook by sending out waves from a single source. These bounce around the oven, off the walls and floor, so they hit the food from different angles. When a dish (especially a deep one) is placed directly on the bottom of the oven, the microwaves have no space to bounce up and hit the bottom of the dish. This means that this part of the dish doesn't cook until conducted heat reaches it from the top and sides. If you are cooking a cake or loaf, the top will be overdone by the time the bottom is cooked.

By elevating the pan on an upturned bowl, microwave rack or plate-stacker, the waves can penetrate the bottom of the pan too and the cake or loaf will cook much more evenly. If you have a microwave corn-popper, its base makes a very good elevating rack.

SAVING POWER USING STANDING TIME

Microwaves are very short waves and their motion is very fast (a very high frequency). When they hit food with water or fat in it — substances where the molecules are relatively free to move around — the waves flow through it at their fast rate and begin to agitate the molecules at high speed. This causes friction, just like the friction if you rub your hands together, which, in turn, generates heat. This is what cooks the food. When the waves stop, the friction goes on with its own momentum and only subsides gradually.

In microwave cooking, this gives rise to an important technique — allowing standing time after microwaving — which enables the food to finish cooking on its own. Make it a practice to take food out when it has not quite finished cooking, while you prepare other parts of the meal. Don't take off the cover — this keeps the heat in and enables the cooking to continue.

Cakes and breads benefit from this, as it prevents the outside becoming overcooked while the middle finishes off.

Protein foods, including cheese, eggs, meat and fish, tend to toughen in the microwave if overcooked. This can be prevented by allowing them to stand, covered, for about half as long again as it took to cook them.

BOILING IN THE MICROWAVE

Any foods which need to be boiled in the microwave, like pasta, rice, jams, and some soups or casseroles, should be put into a dish which seems much too big for the quantity. This allows the mixture to rise high up the sides of the dish (and it will!) without spilling over and messing up the oven.

METAL AND MICROWAVES DON'T MIX

A microwave oven works because the microwaves pass through the food container and into the food. Microwaves can pass through many things but not through metal. (This includes twist-ties, which cause arcing.) They can pass easily through most kinds of plastic, paper, glass and any pottery or china without metal trim, paint or glaze.

TESTING POTTERY AND CHINA FOR USE IN THE MICROWAVE

Metal glazes are not always obvious. While it is easy to see gold lines in a pattern, many metals are ingredients in pottery glazes to give different colours, including reds, blues, greens and browns. Usually the amount of metal in a coloured glaze will not be enough to cause problems, but sometimes the clay itself contains high amounts of iron, especially dark-coloured or speckled clays. If you want to see whether pots or plates you already have are suitable for the microwave oven, try this simple test. Put the empty dish into the microwave with a glass of water and microwave on High for 60 seconds. If the dish becomes noticeably warm or hot it has a high metal content and should not be used in the microwave. (Do not leave the microwave on for longer than 60 seconds without any food or water in it. The waves then bounce back into the magnetron and can eventually burn it out.)

CHOICE OF PLASTIC DISHES IN YOUR MICROWAVE

Dishes with food or drink in them will become hot in the microwave oven because of the contact with hot food. Take care, because of this, in selecting plastic dishes for heating food. Some are perfectly adequate to warm food but will buckle and begin to melt if the food gets very hot, so they should not be used for actual cooking.

When buying plastic microware, look for the microwave-safe symbol on the package and, if you have a combination microwave-convection oven, you will need to ensure that at least some of them are suitable for convection cooking too. There are many on the market which can be used for convection cooking up to 200°C. These are very good if you are cooking with a combination of convection and microwaves.

DISHES FOR MICROWAVING — DEEP OR SHALLOW?

As microwaves penetrate only about 2 – 3 cm into the food, shallow dishes are, in general, preferable to deep ones. Shallow dishes present a greater surface area of food to the microwaves and the food tends to cook faster and more evenly as a result.

In a deeper dish the middle will cook better if the dish is elevated on an upturned bowl, allowing the waves to penetrate from all sides.

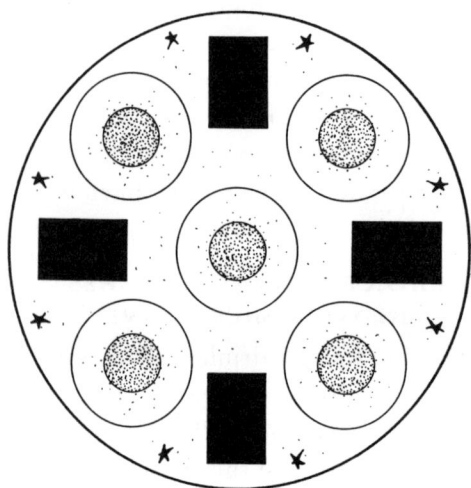

CHOOSING BAKING DISHES FOR YOUR MICROWAVE

For cakes and breads, you need a dish which allows the microwaves to penetrate from all sides to reach right to the centre of the mixture. Round dishes with a central well are especially suitable because they allow the most even cooking. Oblong dishes or round dishes without a well can be used but they will tend to cook the mixture faster at the ends than in the middle so the sides may be overcooked before the middle is done.

FOIL IN THE MICROWAVE

You may have heard that you should never use foil in a microwave. However, you can use the reflective qualities of metal to advantage if your pan is the wrong shape. By binding small, smooth pieces of foil onto the corners of the pan, the microwaves will be reflected off the ends of the dish and thus cook them less than the middle. You can use this technique to shield sensitive or thin pieces of food and prevent them overcooking before the rest is done. Be careful, however, to use only a small amount of foil and not to let it touch the sides of the oven, or it will produce arcing — something like miniature lightning — inside your oven, which can eventually damage the magnetron. If you look into your oven and see blue lights, turn it off and look inside to see what is causing them. Remove the metal which is causing the problem and continue cooking.

ADAPTING CONVENTIONAL RECIPES FOR MICROWAVING

Many of your favourite conventional recipes will adapt well to the microwave if you are prepared to experiment a little. Some will be different from the way you may be used to them but may be just as nice. Unless you are using a browning dish or some pastry-crisping paper, foods will not generally come out with a crisp crust from the microwave. However, a crust can sometimes be added afterwards under the conventional griller. To convert your recipes, follow these simple rules and be prepared to test them once or twice with small variations until you get them the way you want them:

• Reduce the liquid content slightly, as there will be less evaporation in microwaving. If necessary, add more thickening to sauces as well.

• Precook ingredients which take longer to cook (such as rice in stuffed vegetables) in the dish by themselves before adding them to the rest of the dish.

• Cook delicate foods which might otherwise toughen, such as egg dishes and custards, on a lower microwave setting for a little longer rather than on High. The texture will be improved.

• Foods which are uneven in shape or in moisture content will tend to cook unevenly unless they are covered and cooked on a lower power setting. Standing time is important for these foods too.

• Large items, like joints of meat, need to be turned from time to time to allow the microwaves to reach new surfaces of the food.

• Add salt and strong flavourings after cooking. These often taste more concentrated in the microwaved version of a dish and you might need less than normal.

• Dishes which need covering in conventional cooking should be covered for microwaving too. If you do not want a very moist result, cover with paper towel rather than cling wrap or a lid.

• Foods which need constant stirring in convention cooking should be stirred about every minute or two during microwave cooking. Dishes with lots of moisture, like casseroles and soups, also need stirring from time to time during cooking. This prevents them overcooking at the sides and mixes the hot edges into the cooler middle of the dish.

ADAPTING SAUCES FOR THE MICROWAVE

The microwave is the quickest and easiest way to make sauces. There is far less stirring and there are fewer lumps than with conventional methods. It is easy to adapt your favourite sauce recipes for microwave cooking:

• Precook any solid ingredients like mushrooms, onions and prawns, and leave them aside.

• Measure out less liquid than usual, or some extra flour or cornflour. Sauces evaporate less in the microwave and will otherwise come out too runny.

• You can cook a normal flour roux in the microwave if you wish, stirring after each minute. A wire whisk is best for stirring.

• If you prefer, you can eliminate the fat content and use cornflour. Make the cornflour into a paste first with a little of the (cold) liquid in the recipe. Mix in the remaining liquid and microwave it on High in one minute bursts, stirring in between, until it thickens. Then add your flavourings, like cheese, mushrooms or chocolate, and stir well.

• If the sauce is too liquid, mix in a little extra flour or cornflour, made into a paste first. If it is too thick, stir in more liquid.

MICROWAVE TIMES AND WATTAGES

If you try microwave recipes from a book and find that the timings seem to give wrong results consistently, either undercooked or overcooked, the chances are your microwave oven has a different power level (wattage) than the one used to test the recipes in the book. This does not matter because you can adjust the cooking times to suit your oven. To convert a recipe from 500 watts to 600–650 watts, add 10 per cent of the cooking time at the end of cooking. To convert 700 watts back to 600–650 watts, reduce cooking time by 5–10 per cent. Once you have worked out the discrepancy with your own oven, it is easy to adapt all other recipes in the book to suit your equipment.

MICROWAVE SETTINGS: WHICH TO USE?

If you are converting a recipe to microwave for the first time and are uncertain whether to cook the food on full power or to use a lower setting, the rule is similar to conventional cooking. Foods which are apt to toughen, like tougher cuts of meat or fish, heavier types of cake, or egg dishes, are best cooked for a little longer on a lower power setting.

Microwave cooking need not always be quick. It can take hours. Foods which are normally really slow-cooked, like stewing steak, are best cooked very slowly in the microwave too — even simmered gently on Defrost setting. (You may want to give them a short cook on a higher setting first to get them hot and then reduce the heat to simmer them.) The real difference from traditional cooking will be the overall time — usually about half the conventional time or less. If you are unsure of how long a dish will take, allow plenty of time and check occasionally to see how it is cooking. In this way it is really very similar to traditional methods of cooking.

ARRANGING FOOD IN THE MICROWAVE

If you are more familiar with traditional cooking methods, you will find that foods need to be arranged differently in a microwave for best results:
• Arrange foods in a ring in the oven for most even heating.

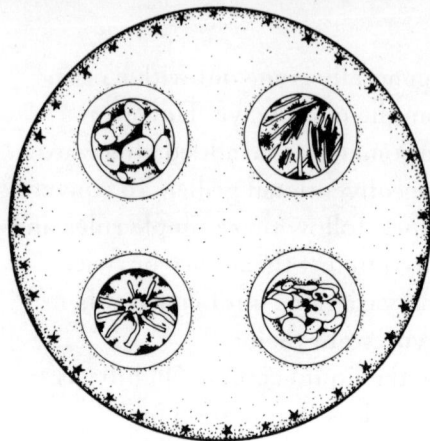

• If your microwave does not have a rotating carousel, turn the food a little several times during the cooking. This exposes a different set of surfaces to the microwaves.

TIMING FOOD IN THE MICROWAVE

Microwave cooking has a different set of timing rules from conventional cooking:
• Remember that, in a microwave, the quantity of food affects the cooking time and a small amount will take less time than a large amount. The time is not necessarily directly proportional to the amount, though, so don't assume that two potatoes will always take twice as long as one. They may need less than twice the amount one would take.
• Always check if a dish is done after the minimum time and continue cooking if necessary. Overcooked microwave dishes may be tough and unpalatable.
• Times given in recipes are usually for ingredients at room temperature, unless stated otherwise. Microwave times, like conventional cooking times, are affected considerably by starting temperature. Frozen food will take longer to cook than its room temperature counterpart as it has further to go to warm up. Make allowances for this when adapting recipes in which you will be using some frozen ingredients.
• When working out cooking times for microwaving new foods, remember that

dense foods (such as meat or potatoes) take much longer to cook than light, porous foods (such as bread or cake).

• Small pieces of food cook much faster than large ones as the microwaves don't have as far to travel to the centre. For faster cooking, cut the food into smaller pieces.

FOODS WHICH DON'T ADAPT TO MICROWAVING

Some dishes do not convert successfully to the microwave:

• Don't try to microwave very large foods, like a 12 kg turkey. These foods cook more efficiently by conventional methods.

• Don't try to microwave very dry foods like popcorn unless you have a special dish or bag for doing it. As it is the moisture in foods which cooks them, very dry foods may not microwave well.

• Don't try to deep fry in the microwave. It is dangerous and can cause burns when you open the oven, not to mention the mess the spattering will cause.

• Don't try to microwave foods which need to develop a good crust, like pancakes or pastries, unless you have a browning dish or some crisping-paper.

• Don't try to boil eggs in their shells (or out of them) without breaking the yolk. They can explode.

WARMING SANDWICHES IN THE MICROWAVE

You can warm sandwiches in the microwave but you need to be careful on two counts. Bread becomes tough if microwaved for too long so the time should be the minimum needed to warm the filling — no more than a minute or two on full power. To prevent the bread becoming soggy underneath, wrap the sandwich in paper towel before cooking it. If the filling is very thick or resistant to heating, it is best to microwave it first, separately, before making up the sandwich.

TACO SHELLS IN A TRICE

Warm taco shells in your microwave in just a minute or two while you prepare the final touches to the fillings.

Stand them on their open edges in a circle on the microwave floor or carousel tray and microwave them at full power for 1–2 minutes. They will be crisp and warm.

TO COVER OR NOT TO COVER

As a rule, you need to cover food in the microwave in about the same circumstances as you would when cooking conventionally. Having said that, it must be pointed out that things occur in the microwave which don't really have a counterpart in conventional cooking. If in doubt, it is usually best to cover foods to promote even heating. Only those foods which must not be soggy should remain uncovered. Here are some guidelines:
• Foods with sauces, or moist foods, such as dips and spreads, should be covered to prevent them drying out and to stop them splattering on the sides of the oven. You can use a microwave-safe plastic cling wrap, a good lid, a plate inverted over the dish, or paper towel.
• Moist vegetables, such as carrots, broccoli, cabbage and beans should be covered, as above. Vegetables cooked in tough skins, like potatoes or pumpkin can be placed as they are on the microwave tray and cooked without covering. (Be sure to prick vegetables with a tough skin thoroughly first to prevent them exploding.)
• Meats to be cooked in any longer, slower process, like chicken joints or casseroles, should be covered with wrap or a lid.
• Meats to be cooked rare or very quickly, (such as veal or beef steaks) should not be covered, especially if you are using a browning dish.
• Foods that are moist but not wet, like sandwiches or onions can be covered with a paper towel. This will keep them moist, but not allow the steam to condense into

water dribbles which would make the food soggy.
• Bakery foods, such as bread, pastry or pancakes, should not be covered or they will become soggy. They should never be cooked for very long as they become hard.

MICROWAVE THAWING OF FROZEN FOODS

The microwave cooker is a marvellous adjunct to the freezer, but thawing food is not simply a matter of putting it in the microwave and turning it on.

First, remove any metal packaging. This might be anything from a wrapper to a twist tie. Flat foil trays can usually be put on the floor of the microwave but if you are in doubt refer to the microwave manufacturer's instructions.

Microwave-safe plastic wrapping can remain and is usually helpful in collecting melting juices from the food. If there is a likelihood of these leaking, put the frozen food in a microwave-safe dish. If the food is not wrapped at this stage it is best to cover it with wrap or with a lid to prevent it drying.

Use a low setting on the microwave oven if you have one. If you have only one setting, try turning the microwave on in 10- or 15-second bursts with pauses of 2–3 minutes in between.

Keep a check on the food as it thaws. Unless it is a very small or flat item, food usually needs to be turned over, stirred or separated as it begins to thaw to expose new frozen surfaces to the microwaves. Otherwise, you can end up with food which is partly cooked on the outside and still frozen underneath. Turn and separate the pieces several times and microwave them again.

Always make sure that large cuts of meat or whole poultry are thoroughly thawed and rinsed before you start to cook them. (Rinsing removes stale blood which can carry bacteria.) If they are still frozen in the centre, they may not cook through, although the dish may look cooked from the outside. Apart from this being unpalatable, it creates a danger that any food poisoning bacteria present (although normally killed in cooking) might be alive and well in the centre of the meat.

CATERING GUIDE

PRESENTATION AND GARNISHING

CLEAR SOUPS THAT SPARKLE

For everyday fare, the family probably appreciates home-made soup for its flavour without worrying whether it is clear or murky. For entertaining, though, it is good to be able to serve a soup which not only tastes good, but also looks beautiful.

To achieve that final clarity:
• Line a colander with cotton wool or with several layers of paper towel. Strain the soup through this to remove the finer particles; or
• Put some crushed egg-shells and a little egg white into the soup and boil gently for five minutes or so. Strain out the egg white and shells and the soup should come through clear.

DECORATING THE CHEESE BOARD

After a rich meal, while some people are ready for a taste of strong cheese, others prefer to pick at something light and refreshing. Here is a way they can do both. Put some grapes (black and white for the best display) into the freezer the day before you want them. Prepare the cheese plate and, at the last minute, take the grapes from the freezer and place them around the cheese. They will gather a light layer of frost on the surface, which is most attractive, and are deliciously firm (but not hard) to eat in their frozen condition.

FLEURONS

These little crescent-shaped puff pastries make an attractive decoration for hot dishes with rich sauces. They can be made in advance and stored in an airtight container when cool.

Roll out a sheet of ready-made puff pastry. Choose 2 glasses or round fluted biscuit cutters of different sizes, one for the inside and one for the outside edge. Using the smaller cutter, press it, at an angle, onto the surface so that it only cuts half a circle. Use the bigger cutter to make a second cut inside the first, making a crescent shape. When all the fleurons are cut, bake them at 200°C for 3–5 minutes or until they are golden and well-risen.

GARNISHING A MORNAY

Mornays can be garnished in many ways to relieve their tendency to look a little bland and pale:
• Scatter grated, sliced or crumbled cheese on top and bake or place the dish

under a hot grill until it browns and bubbles.

• Sprinkle it with paprika, nutmeg and/or parsley.

• Sprinkle it with breadcrumbs (or breadcrumbs mixed with some parmesan cheese) at the beginning of cooking and bake it until it browns and toasts.

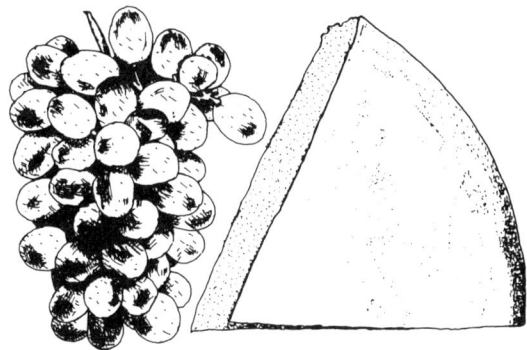

• Slice tomato onto the top of the sauce (with or without cheese or breadcrumbs) at the beginning of cooking and allow it to toast onto the surface while cooking.

• Make a scone mixture and decorate the dish with small, shaped pieces of this before cooking. The mixture will cook with the dish.

MAKING ASPIC

Aspic is simply jelly with a savoury base, used to set cold savoury foods or, on its own, chopped up with a knife or in a food processor, to decorate the edges of cold platters.

Jelly can be obtained from three basic sources. Gelatine, the most common, is traditionally made from calves' feet, simmered in water. These days, most of it is made from animal or fish bones. For those who prefer a vegetable source of jelly, Agar-agar, prepared from seaweed, is much the same as gelatine but is more expensive. Isinglass, the finest and most expensive form of jelly-setting agent, is made from parts of the sturgeon (a fish).

To make aspic you will need a quantity of very clear meat, vegetable or fish stock, completely free of fat. (Instructions for clarifying stocks and for removing fat are given elsewhere in this book.) Soak the gelatine for a while in a little of the cold liquid before stirring it into the hot remainder.

If the aspic is to be used as a garnish, allow it to set thoroughly and then chop it carefully, making sure the knife, board and your hands (or the food processor) are free of grease. Grease will cloud the aspic.

If it is to be used as a coating over cold food, chill it until it just starts to form a light gel. Have the food to be coated really cold. Spoon the jelly gradually over the food, until it is coated. In hot weather, have a bowl of ice cubes beside you and chill individual spoonfuls of aspic jelly against the ice until they are just ready to set, before applying them to the food. A quicker but less attractive finish can be obtained by pouring over the slightly set aspic and brushing it in place with a very clean (degreased in hot water) pastry brush.

If it is for setting a composite dish in a mould, chill the mould and pour a little aspic into it, swishing it around to make a light coating on the side. Chill it until it sets and repeat the process if you need to build up the thickness of the layer a little. Arrange the food in the mould a layer at a time, covering each with aspic as it is completed and leaving it to set in the fridge. In this way the dish is gradually built up. If the unused portion of the aspic sets before you get around to using it, warm it again slightly. (A microwave is good here.) It should be just on the point of setting, but not yet set, when it is added to the dish.

MELBA TOAST

Melba toast — delicate, thin toast slices — is a natural accompaniment for home made pâtés or terrines at a dinner party. The commercially-prepared variety tends to be somewhat hard and dry but if you have ever tried to slice fresh bread into thin enough slices you may feel there is no option. In fact, delicious Melba toast can be made from your household bread, white or brown as you prefer.

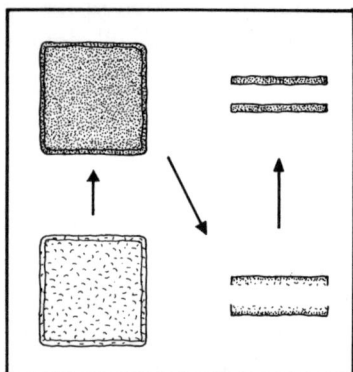

Simply use a thin sliced loaf of fresh bread. Make normal toast from half as many slices as you wish to end up with. Cut the crusts off the toasted slices and, with a very sharp knife, slice down through the soft middle of the toast, between the toasted sides. You now have two thin slices of bread, toasted on one side only. Toast the raw sides and, presto, beautiful fresh Melba Toast.

POTATO NESTS

A decorative touch for a special meal is to serve individual nests of fried potato in which the meat or seafood can be set very attractively.

To make the nests you need two small metal sieves, one a little larger than the other, and a deep frying pan.

Grate the raw potatoes. A food processor is good for this. Put the grated potato into a large colander and rinse it under cold running water. Turn it out onto one half of a clean tea towel, fold the other half over it and pat it dry.

Heat some oil for deep-frying. Divide the shredded potato into the number of portions you will need. Spread the first portion out in the larger sieve and then press the smaller one into it, enclosing the 'nest'. Immerse the whole thing in the oil and fry until the potato is golden brown. Turn out the nest and repeat until you have made enough. Drain the nests on paper towel until you are ready to use them.

VEGETABLE GARNISHES

Fresh salad vegetables make excellent garnishes for just about any savoury dish. Cut in various decorative ways, they add colour and texture — not to mention good nutrition — to the dishes they adorn.

Cucumbers

Cucumbers can be prepared in many ways. Here are a few:
• Cut them in thin slices and make one straight cut from the side to the centre. Twist each cut radius edge a different way and stand them on the opening.

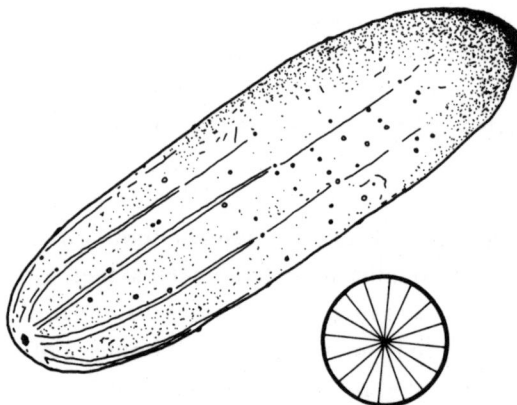

• Score the outside of the cucumber with a fork in parallel lines. Slice it thinly.

• Cut a piece of cucumber about 2–3 cm long. With a sharp knife, make a spiral cut which reaches into the centre of the cucumber and continues down its length. The parallel rings of the spiral should be about 2–3 mm apart. Open out the spiral.

Radishes

Radishes make beautiful flower shapes. Cut them in one of the following ways and then leave them in a bowl of water in the fridge for an hour or so. The 'petals' will open out during that time:

• Cut off the stalk and cut a thin slice off the opposite end, making a small white round. Starting from the top end, just outside the white round you have cut off, make a cut down the side which stops just short of the stem end. Make another opposite this one and then one each side between these — 4 cuts in all in a square shape. The partly-cut pieces on the sides will form the petals.

• Cut off the stalk. Starting at the other end, cut right down the middle of the radish, stopping just short of the stem. Make another cut at right angles to this one, then another 2 diagonally across these. You will have 8 petals which will open out in the water.

Celery

Celery will curl just like radishes in a bowl of water in the fridge. Cut off lengths of 8–10 cm. Make parallel cuts about 4–5 mm apart down the length of each piece, stopping just short of the end each time. These will curl outwards in the water.

SWEET GARNISHES

Chocolate decoration

A rich cake or dessert can look very dramatic with chocolate decoration:

• Put some dark cooking chocolate in the fridge until it is hard. Grate it (or use a food processor) to a coarse powder.

• Sprinkle it in a spiral over the surface of the dish or dredge it from a coarse sieve. (Make sure it stays cool or it will begin to go into lumps and clog the sieve.)

• For a really decorative effect, sit a paper lace doily with plenty of cut-out space in it on top of the cake and sift a small amount of the chocolate on top (you can use powdered cocoa if you prefer). Then carefully remove the paper and the chocolate will be left in a pattern.

• You can also crumble a Flake bar onto the top of the dish or scrape curls of chocolate off a firm but not hard chocolate bar with a potato peeler.

• Put some rose leaves in the freezer while you melt some chocolate in the microwave or on the stove. Wipe only one side of

each leaf across the chocolate and sit them, leaf side down, on a sheet of waxed paper or plastic freezer sheets on a tray. If necessary, put them in the fridge briefly to harden, then peel off the leaves.

• Spread some melted chocolate onto a laminex or plastic board and leave it to set in a cool place. Use a long-bladed sharp knife to shave off curls of chocolate, in a diagonal sawing movement along the surface, holding the knife nearly upright.

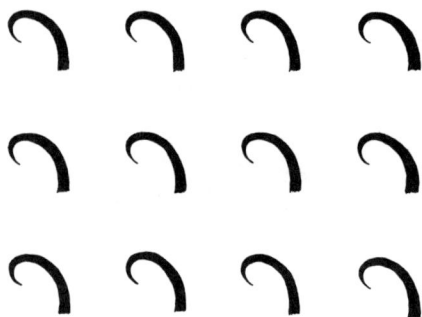

Cutting marshmallows

Marshmallows are excellent for decorating fruit, cream or ice-cream desserts, and even for beating into fillings and toppings to make them light. However, they can be difficult to handle as they tend to stick to the knife and the finger. To reduce this problem, wet the knife and your fingers in cold water before you tackle them.

Sugar decoration

Sometimes you want the table to look just that bit more festive and you might look for ways to dress it up a little. Here is one idea which can be used with adult groups but is especially good with children.

Mix a drop or two of food colouring into a tablespoon or two of caster sugar and allow it to dry a little. Dip the rims of drinking glasses in egg white and then into the sugar mixture. They should pick up a fine layer all around. You can use any leftover sugar to decorate biscuits, or dip grapes into the egg white and then into the sugar for a decorative frosted effect.

TEMPTING TREATS AND SNIPPETS

SIMPLE DELIGHTS TO SERVE WITH COFFEE

A simple-to-make and different treat to serve with coffee after a special meal is chocolate-covered fruits. You will need a block of cooking chocolate (plain or milk, or some of each) and a collection of fresh and preserved fruits. Any fruit which is not too wet in texture can be used, such as fresh strawberries, thick banana slices, brandied prunes, raisins, crystallised ginger and dried apricots.

Cut the fruit, if necessary, into bite-sized pieces and stick a toothpick into each piece. Put a sheet of freezer plastic on a cold metal tray. (Put it in the freezer for a few minutes before you start.)

Melt the chocolate in the microwave, or in a bowl over hot water in a saucepan. (Use 2 bowls if you want some milk and some plain chocolate.) Allow it to cool a little but not to the point of setting. The chocolate should still be melted enough to coat the fruit. Dip each fruit piece, holding it by its toothpick, into the chocolate and lift it out, allowing any drips to fall back into the dish. Place the chocolates on the waiting plastic sheet. As the sheet is filled, put it in the fridge for a few minutes to firm up. When cold, the chocolates will peel off the plastic sheet and can be arranged on a serving dish.

CHRISTMAS PUDDING CHOCOLATES

Banish forever those hours you spend wondering what to do with the leftover Christmas pudding. These chocolates are guaranteed to disappear in no time flat.

Crumble the pudding into a bowl and pour over a generous quantity of brandy. (If you are catering for children, you might prefer to use concentrated fruit juice.) Mix with enough of the fluid to get the consistency of chocolate truffles. Take out spoonfuls of the mixture and shape them into balls, placing them in rows on greaseproof paper on a baking sheet. Put them in the freezer for a few hours until they are quite cold and firm.

Spread some greaseproof paper over a chilled baking tray. Melt some dark cooking chocolate in the microwave or over a bowl of water on the cooktop. Remove the pudding centres from the freezer and, one at a time, spear them with a toothpick and dip them into the warm chocolate. Place each one on the prepared tray and remove its toothpick. Decorate the top immediately with a piece of crystallised ginger or a nut. They will set quickly as the pudding is still cold.

A SPECIAL CHEESE BALL

A spectacular and delicious table centre (also a lovely 'take-a-plate' dish) can be made very quickly and simply with the help of a food processor and a microwave oven. (You can make it without them but it will mean a little more time and trouble.)

• Place about 1 cup of ricotta or neufchâtel cheese and 1 cup of roughly chopped up smoked or blue cheese in a bowl in the microwave and cook them on High for a minute or less, until they are soft enough to mix together.

• Grate about 1 cup of strong cheddar cheese and mix this with the other cheeses.

• Mix in 1 cup of assorted, chopped ingredients from the list below (or your own), together with some herbs and spices, according to taste:
crumbled fried bacon, walnuts, gherkins (drained), capers (drained), pickled onions (drained), celery
VARIATION: add a spoonful or two of mayonnaise or seafood dressing and:
shredded tuna, cooked prawns, shredded crabmeat, chives, chopped capsicum, cooked mushrooms
VARIATION: use ricotta and neufchâtel or cream cheese with a dash of brandy and:
coconut, crystallised ginger, dried fruits, candied peel, glacé cherries, coconut/nuts

• Chill the mixture in a plastic bag in the fridge for an hour or in the freezer for ¼ – ½ an hour until it is firm enough to shape.

• Meanwhile, make a mixture to coat the ball. This might be:
Chopped nuts mixed with herbs or fresh, chopped parsley
Toasted chopped almonds and coconut mixed with a little finely-chopped crystallised ginger for a sweet cheese ball
Poppy seeds and black pepper or spices
Sesame seeds

• Form the chilled cheese into a ball and roll it in the prepared coating. For best results, chill overnight or at least for a few hours before serving to allow the flavours and textures to mingle.

FILL SAVOURIES LAST

Generally, it is best not to fill cooked pastry cases with moist fillings until just before guests are due to arrive, or they will become soggy. For the same reason, moist toppings should never be put onto toast or biscuit bases until close to the time people are due. If you have to prepare them in advance, perhaps to allow aspic to set over them, keep the time between preparation and eating to a minimum and spread a little butter or cream cheese over the toast or biscuit before adding the moist topping. This stops the base from absorbing water too quickly.

AFTERNOON TEA WITH STRAWBERRIES

For a springtime afternoon tea (or morning coffee) treat to serve to guests, try this fresh and decorative idea. You will need a packet of puffed, toast-style cracker biscuits, a punnet of strawberries, a carton of ricotta or cream cheese, a kiwi fruit or two and a few passionfruit.

Cut the biscuits into bite-sized pieces with a sharp, serrated knife. Wash and hull the strawberries and cut any large ones into smaller pieces. Peel and slice the kiwi fruit and scoop the passionfruit into a bowl.

Spread each biscuit with a little cheese. Top with a slice of kiwi fruit, a strawberry (or piece of strawberry) and then a teaspoon of passionfruit. Serve as soon as possible, before the biscuits become soft.

A SPECIAL NO-COOK PARTY CAKE

For this cake you will need one or two packets of gingernut biscuits or plain chocolate-flavoured biscuits (without icing or chocolate on top). Whip a carton of cream with some fine sugar until it is light.

Line a large, flat platter or biscuit tray with greaseproof paper or freezer wrap. Spread a layer of the cream in it and then lay a biscuit on it at one end. Spread some cream on this and then put another on top of it. Build up a stack in this way, about 4–5 biscuits high. Spread a little cream on the side of the first stack, facing the empty part of the dish. Build another pile, butted up to the first one, and then more piles in a row until the dish is filled. Keep the piles more or less the same height. Make sure you reserve enough cream to spread over the outside of the long pile of biscuit stacks.

Cover the cake lightly with plastic to prevent it drying out and put it in the fridge overnight to set. During this time, the biscuits will absorb moisture from the cream, turning the whole thing into a cake which can be cut through in slices. Sprinkle the top of the cake with chocolate flakes or chopped crystallised ginger before serving.

A FUN DRINK FOR CHILDREN

It is amazing how children are attracted to food and drink which is brightly coloured. Put some vegetable dye into the most ordinary food which they would otherwise not touch, and more often than not they will lap it up.

You can use this to advantage at children's parties. The simplest way is to make up some jugs of fruit juice or cordial and boost their colour vividly with different vegetable dyes (these are healthier than chemical dyes).

If it is very hot and you have more time to spare, make up some trays of ice cubes or ice-balls in different colours, using vegetable dyes. Pile assorted coloured cubes into tall glasses and top up with lemonade.

SUCCESSFUL TOFFEE

If your toffee is gritty, the chances are that the children will like it anyway but the adults might prefer a finer texture.

Grittiness is caused by the sugar crystallising in the mixture. It will do this if the heat is too high and the water boils before the sugar dissolves completely. It may also happen if the heat is too low and too much water evaporates before the sugar is dissolved. If you have this problem, increase the amount of water in the recipe next time and be prepared to stir the liquid at a simmer for slightly longer.

CATERING FOR LARGE NUMBERS

BULK BREWING OF TEA

These days, the problem of making large amounts of tea is usually taken care of by tea bags, which allow individuals to make their own cup to their own taste. Even if you are making a bulk pot, tea bags can give you more control over the result. However, it is sometimes more economical to use leaf tea and some people still feel that the flavour is better. In these cases, it can be a problem to make the tea strong enough for the first cups to be enjoyable but not so strong that the later ones will taste stewed. The tannin in the tea is the culprit and will keep leaching out of the leaves while they remain steeping. The answer can be to make your own 'tea bag' by putting the required amount of tea leaves into a clean muslin bag on a string and dangling it into the pot. When the tea has steeped enough, you can remove the bag and prevent the tea from getting stronger. It helps with the washing up, too, and the leaves are nicely packaged for scattering on the garden.

CATERING QUANTITIES

If you are not used to feeding large numbers of people it can be very difficult to know how much of everything to supply for a party. (If in doubt, always err on the generous side. It is easier to use up leftovers than to apologise for running out.) Here are some guidelines to help. For each item, multiply the amount per portion by the number of people to work out the amount to buy. (A calculator is helpful.) For convenience, the amounts for about 20 people are given as an example throughout.

Drinks

•WINE: One bottle of wine serves 6 average glasses. Allow about 1 bottle of each type of wine per 4 people.
•FORTIFIED WINES: You will get 12–16 glasses of sherry, vermouth or port per bottle.
•SPIRITS: One bottle of spirits should provide 30 cocktails or ⅔ of that when taken only with mixers or neat. Liqueurs normally give about 30 drinks per bottle.
•CORDIALS: One bottle of cordial is usually about enough for 20 drinks.
•COFFEE: You generally need to allow about 25–50% more cups of coffee than people to cater for second and third cups (depending on how long and relaxed the event is to be). Allow about 10 g ground coffee or 2–3 g instant, 200 ml of water and about 20–25 ml milk per cup. Sugar varies considerably according to how many people take it but allow about 1 teaspoon or two lumps of sugar per person. (For 20 cups, this means about 200 g ground coffee, about 4 litres of water, about 400–500 ml milk and 500 g sugar. If you are using instant coffee you will need about 70 g.)
•TEA: Again, allow about 25–50% more cups than people. You will need about 2–3 g tea leaves or 1 tea bag per person, and about 200 ml water and 15 ml milk. (For 20 cups, this means about 70 g tea or 20 tea bags, 4 litres water, 300 ml milk and 500 g sugar.)

Food

- BREAD AND BUTTER: For each slice of bread you will need about 6–7g of softened butter or margarine per person (1 large sandwich loaf and about 120–140 g butter for 20 people). This also serves as an indication for sandwich making. 20 rounds of sandwiches (one round is two slices of bread with filling in between them) will need 2 large loaves and 250–300 g butter.

  If you are using rolls, you will need one each plus a few spares for seconds, with about twice as much butter as for sliced bread (about 250 g softened butter per 20 people).

- MEAT SANDWICHES: To make meat sandwiches, allow about 30–50 g of meat per sandwich. This means that 500 g of thinly-sliced meat will make about 10–15 sandwiches. The filling can be bulked out by adding sliced tomato, shredded lettuce or alfalfa.

- HARD-BOILED EGGS: To make sandwiches from hard-boiled eggs, allow 2 eggs per 3 sandwiches, with butter and mayonnaise to moisten. This means about 14 eggs per 20 sandwiches.

- PASTRY: Allow ½ kg of pastry per 50 small or 2 large tarts or flans.

- SOUPS: Allow about 200–250 ml per person (about a gallon for 25 people). Don't make portions too large or you will spoil people's appetite for the rest of the meal.

- PÂTÉ STARTERS: You will need about 40–60 g per person with 1 slice of toast each (cut into 4 triangles) and some shredded lettuce. For 20 people, allow about 1 kg of pâté and half a large lettuce.

- SEAFOOD STARTERS: Allow about 30 g of shell-less seafood per person with lettuce and a dressing. Shellfish bought in the shell yields only about half its weight when shelled. This means, for example,

that 1 kg of prawns will provide about ½ kg of prawn meat and make about 16 prawn cocktails.

- FISH MAIN COURSE: When catering with whole fish, as much as half the weight can be in the head and bone. Allow about 300–400 g of whole large fish per person. A fish of about ½ kg will usually do nicely between two people and smaller ones may need to be served one for each person. Fillets involve little waste and 150–200 g each should be sufficient.

- MEAT OR POULTRY: For a sit-down meal, allow up to 250–300 g of meat on the bone per person (depending on how much bone) or about 125–175 g of boneless meat. (This includes cold sliced meats or pâtés for salad.) You can allow a little less for a buffet where there is a greater variety of dishes. For smaller poultry, allow 1 joint per person for a buffet or 2 for a sit-down meal.

- SALAD: Although salads can have many different components, allow per person about ⅙ lettuce, 2 cm of cucumber, 1 tomato, 30 g shredded cabbage, ¼ carrot, 60 g potatoes, 2 tbsp alfalfa or bean sprouts or equivalent vegetables. This means that you will need about 3 lettuces, 1–2 cucumbers, 1 ½ kg tomatoes, 600 g cabbage, 1 kg carrots, 1 ½ kg potatoes and about 2 punnets of sprouts.

- RICE OR PASTA: Allow about 45–50 g uncooked rice per person or about 1 kg rice for 20 people. (If possible, cook the rice the previous day and reheat it in the microwave or in the oven just before serving.)

- FRUIT SALAD: You will need about 125 g fruit per person or about 2 ½ kg for 20 people. Allow about 750 ml cream or plain yoghurt to serve with it.

- CHEESE: For an end-of-meal course, you will need about 40–50 g per person or about 1 kg for 20 people. However, the more different types you have, the more people will eat, as they will want to sample several. This means catering with slightly larger quantities. As a cocktail nibble, you will need about twice as much. Allow about 1 kg of biscuits for 20 people.

BUFFET CATERING

Buffets are an excellent and easy way to feed a large number of people. There is no need to try to arrange tables where everyone can sit, or to find sufficient matching tableware, if this is a problem. Nor do you have the ordeal of serving numerous plates of food, or watching people's food get cold while they wait for everyone to be served.

But there are still traps. If you are preparing a buffet meal, it is important to remember that everyone will usually want to sample a bit of everything. It is therefore more sensible to prepare a large amount of a few dishes than to prepare lots of smaller dishes. You will certainly run out of at least some dishes before everyone has had their turn if you try to cater with lots of variety and, overall, people will eat more. If possible, place more than one platter of a particular dish on the table, a good distance away from one another, so more people can help themselves to it at once. This also makes the table look generously laden and attractive.

HEALTH AND SAFETY IN THE KITCHEN

BURNS - PREVENTION AND FIRST AID

PLACING OF SAUCEPANS ON THE STOVE

Small children have a fascination with things they can grab and pull. In a confined kitchen adults, too, might have problems with things sticking out into the walking area. In either case, saucepan handles which stick out into the walking area are a hazard. Children can grab them and pull them down, spilling the contents over themselves. You might brush past them accidentally yourself and knock the contents over your legs and feet. In either case, serious burns can occur.

To prevent this type of accident, always use back plates on a stove in preference to front plates and position saucepans with their handles out of harm's way, toward the side or the back of the stove. Avoid placing a handle where it can become hot from another burner or plate as this can also cause burns, not to mention damage to the saucepan handle.

LIFTING HOT PANS

One of the greatest hazards in the kitchen is moving hot, heavy pans from one place to another. This is especially dangerous when they are coming from or going to an oven which is high; at eye-level, for instance. This makes balancing the dish difficult.

To minimise the risks, always have the destination prepared before you lift the pan, and make sure you have a clear route to it. If there is someone else in the kitchen, warn them you are about to move a dangerous pan.

Use good oven gloves to hold the dish. NEVER hold a pan with a wet cloth or glove: the water will transmit the heat to your hand and burn you.

Keep the lid on the pot to ensure that you won't be burned by rising steam.

USING OVEN GLOVES

Oven gloves should be chosen with care because they are all that is between you and a potentially serious burn or accident.

Make sure they are made of a thick, well-insulated fabric which will give you sufficient time to put a dish down before it becomes hot. The fabric should also be non-slip and resistant to heat. Avoid gloves which are thick on only one side unless they can only be put on the right way around. If you put these on the wrong way around, you could burn yourself.

You should be able to open your thumb and fingers wide enough to grasp a large pan without exposing part of your hand to its surface. You should also be able to separate your hands from each other far enough not to feel awkward with a large pan.

STEAM BURNS FROM OPENING DISHES

Dishes which have been cooking with a cover or lid, especially those in the microwave, can build up a considerable amount of steam inside. For safety's sake, always remove the cover from a hot pan with the opening facing away from you at first, to allow the scalding steam to escape safely. Then lift the rest of the cover.

BURNS FROM FRYING

Frying brings the possibility of burns from hot fat, especially if moist or wet foods are put into the pan. Fat also spatters from browning meat, especially if the meat is wet or bleeds into the fat.

To reduce the risk, take the pan off the heat when you add the food. Make sure the food is as dry as possible — water spatters badly when it meets hot fat. Never drop food in from a great height because it will splash when it reaches the fat. Instead, lower it gently, flat to the pan, and let it go just above the surface of the fat. Use tongs or a spoon to lower in food to avoid putting your hands near the fat.

Use a large, deep pan for frying and, if necessary, wear a garment with sleeves. Using a large pan will also help to reduce the amount of spattered fat to be cleaned off the cooker afterwards.

BURNS FIRST AID

Mild burns should be treated immediately with ice or cold running water. Keep the burnt area in the water or against a bag of frozen vegetables until it stops stinging — at least 2 minutes.

Never put fats, like butter or margarine, on a burn. They don't help the burn and they attract germs which can cause infection.

Serious burns, those which actually remove the skin, should receive immediate medical help. Don't put anything on them as this will tear away more of the damaged tissue.

KITCHEN HYGIENE — KEY TO FAMILY HEALTH

BIVALVE SHELLFISH: SAFE TO EAT

Bivalve shellfish — all the creatures like oysters, mussels, cockles, abalone and scallops, with two-part shells — are among the best of foods when they are fresh but they are easily contaminated.

The commonest problem is salmonella poisoning, which causes vomiting and diarrhoea. This can be avoided by making sure that the shellfish you eat is fresh and clean, and by cooking it. If you are ever unsure about the source of the fish, don't eat it raw. Cooked, it is usually safe.

Some molluscs which are traditionally cooked in their shells, like mussels and clams, should only be eaten if the shells open during cooking. Any which don't open are suspect and should be thrown away.

SAFE MEALS FROM LEFTOVER MEAT

Meat left over from a meal can be recycled in many ways provided that some simple health rules are followed:

• Keep it in a covered container in the fridge until you are ready to use it (and only for a few days at most — your nose will tell you how long) or freeze it.

• Bring it rapidly to high temperature when cooking (boil the mixture or fry it in a very hot pan) and then turn the heat down to simmer. Cooking for ten minutes or more kills bacteria which can otherwise cause food poisoning.

TASTING BOWLS FOR BETTER HYGIENE

Most cooks like to taste food as it nears completion to see if the flavouring needs to be adjusted. Doing this with a spoon has several disadvantages. Either you are left with a lot of spoons to wash up or you could pass any germs you may have around the family (or guests) by putting the spoon back into the food after putting it in your mouth.

If the food is very hot, you will often burn your mouth if you taste straight from the pot. Not only is this painful but the full flavour of the food doesn't come through.

Instead, try using a tasting cup. Any small cup will do — the type used to serve soy sauce in Asian meals is ideal. Spoon a little of the food into the cup and, if necessary, leave it to cool before tasting it. You can eat or drink the sample from the cup without contaminating the spoon you dipped into the dish. This way you can sample hygienically as often as you like.

COVER CUTS AND WOUNDS

Cuts on your hands can easily become infected if they are in contact with perishable foods. Even in a clean kitchen there are bacteria in the air and on most surfaces.

If you cut your hand in the kitchen, it is a good idea to wash it immediately and cover the wound with a waterproof dressing. If you don't have a waterproof one, use a rubber glove or a 'finger cot' (available from chemists). Cloth bandages and ordinary adhesive plasters attract germs as you continue to handle food.

ELECTRIC SHOCK

Never handle electric appliances or plugs with wet hands. Always keep electric cords in good repair and well attached to the appliance. No bare wires should be visible through frayed ends of cords. If the wires touch, the whole appliance could become live, or if you touched the wires, you could.

If someone suffers electric shock in the kitchen (or anywhere else for that matter), *never* try to touch them if they are still in contact with the source of the electricity. First, turn it off at the source, preferably with a rubber glove or plastic implement, or, if that is not possible, turn off the power at the mains. Only then is it safe to touch the victim. If the victim is unconscious, you may need to give mouth-to mouth resuscitation and get medical help.

A minor shock may cause only discomfort and, perhaps, a slight burn. A good sit down afterwards will help. Never give alcohol to people suffering from any kind of shock. This will actually make things worse. A hot cup of sweet tea is better.

NUTRITION BASICS

The three basic nutrients which we all need are protein — the building material of the body; carbohydrate — its chief fuel source; and fat — a concentrated energy source and carrier of fat-soluble vitamins. A healthy eating plan should contain plenty of fruit and vegetables (a good proportion of them uncooked to retain maximum nutrients) and whole-grain foods, and less refined sugar, salt, animal products and chemical food additives than many people are used to.

A diet like this will generally give you all the vitamins and minerals you need too. Vitamins are 'trace elements': foods which are required in only minute amounts for the proper working of the body. Some need to be eaten every day while others can be stored for a long time. Some are carried in the water in foods, some in fats, and one can even come from the effects of sun on the skin. All vitamins are essential but some can be harmful if you have too much of them, while others are just excreted. If your vitamin intake comes entirely in the food you eat, it is not really possible to consume harmful quantities of vitamins.

Minerals are naturally present in the body and need to be replenished by our food. Again, some can be harmful in overdose although they are essential in smaller amounts. They have many roles in the body, from helping the blood to carry oxygen (iron) to hardening the skeleton (calcium). Like vitamins, they help the body to carry out certain tasks and, in fact, they work with vitamins in doing certain jobs.

In a well-balanced diet you are unlikely to have much difficulty getting enough minerals for normal good health.

Most authorities now agree that eating foods raw is better than eating them cooked, because maximum nutrients are retained. However, cutting up fruit and vegetables well before you are ready to eat them can result in some of the more sensitive vitamins, like C, disappearing into the air. If you are going to cook fruit or vegetables, and if you do not want to pour vitamins down the drain, cook them as little as possible and avoid using more water than you need.

YOUR QUICK REFERENCE NUTRIENT CHART

NUTRIENT	FOUND IN	IMPORTANT FOR	COMMENTS
Protein	Meat, fish, eggs, dairy products, grains, pulses.	Building and repairing body tissues, muscles.	Animal source foods are usually 'whole'; vegetables and proteins may need mixing (grain and pulse) to be complete.
Carbohydrate	Grains, fruit, vegetables, dairy products.	Providing the body with fuel for all functions; can be stored as fat.	Can be sugar or starch. Refined sugar provides a quick energy burst and then rebound hunger. Starch takes longer to digest and satisfies longer.
Fibre	Whole-grains, fruit, vegetables	Digestion; carries some vitamins and minerals.	Removed when carbohydrates are refined. Sometimes added again later in processing.
Fats and oils	Meats, fish, eggs, dairy products, grains, nuts, some vegetables, especially pulses.	Energy; conditioning bones, teeth, tissues and skin; protecting vital organs; body insulation; carrying and helping in use of fat-soluble vitamins.	Can be 'saturated' (generally solid at room temperature) and found in animal products, or 'unsaturated' (generally liquid unless chemically treated) and found in vegetable products. Saturated fats contain cholesterol which is needed by the body but can be harmful to people with excessive levels in their blood.
Vitamin A	Many foods, including milk fat (butter, cream); cheese; eggs; animal and fish liver; bright-coloured fruit or vegetables such as carrots, pumpkin, spinach, broccoli, apricots, pawpaw, melons, nectarines.	Growth; conditioning skin and membranes; digestion of protein; good vision.	Availability actually increased by cooking; fat-soluble so not lost in cooking water. Excess is stored in liver and can be harmful. Need to eat some fat to be able to use this vitamin.

YOUR QUICK REFERENCE NUTRIENT CHART

Nutrient	Found in	Important for	Comments
Vitamin B Complex	Plant foods, especially whole-grains, yeast, nuts, liver, milk, meat, fish.	Digestion, metabolism, healthy nervous system.	A group of vitamins usually found together. Water-soluble, so easily lost in cooking water; damaged by heat. Unlikely to eat excess in food but excess in pill form is harmful to nerves.
Vitamin C	Many fruit, especially citrus, berries, rock-melon, pawpaw, capsicum, tomato, potato, leafy vegetables.	Helping body's immune system; healing wounds, maintaining skin, bones, ligaments, brain; coping with stress; digestion, metabolism.	Some doubt about whether huge doses handle infections better than normal doses. Not stored in body and easily destroyed by heat, drying, exposing cut surfaces of fruit to air, long storage. Water-soluble. Works better in presence of B vitamins.
Vitamin D	Plant and animal foods, especially fish-liver oil, oily fish, eggs, dairy products, sunlight.	Maintaining bones, nerves, blood-clotting, heart action.	Fat-soluble, hard not to get enough in a sunny climate. Harmful in excess, contributing to kidney stones and high blood pressure.
Vitamin E	Vegetable/seed oils, whole-grain nuts, soybeans, whole milk products.	Helping fight cancer; blood clots; improving blood-flow; helping blood to carry oxygen; protecting lungs and skin; helping sexual/reproductive functions, vision, healing of wounds.	Fat-soluble group of substances. Can be stored in liver; harmful in large amounts (can raise blood pressure). Easily destroyed by poor storage, chlorine, air pollution.
Vitamin K	Kelp, alfalfa, green vegetables, milk, eggs, vegetable oils, nuts, wheat germ.	Helping blood-clotting; liver function.	A natural preservative; can be made by the body, especially when yoghurt is eaten (because of special yoghurt bacteria). Fat-soluble. Destroyed by poor storage.

FAT REDUCTION
IN YOUR DIET

FAT-FREE STIR FRY

Chinese food can be a delicious addition to a low-fat diet. Stir-fried vegetables, meats and fish stay crisp and lose fewer vitamins than when cooked by some more conventional Western methods. But traditional stir-fried food uses lots of oil and this might not be acceptable in your diet.

You can still get much the same effect, however, without the fat. Substitute some stock or water for the oil and cook in the same way. You may need to cook the food slightly longer and add more water or stock if it disappears, but the result will be just as tasty and much healthier.

REMOVING THE FAT FROM STOCKS, SOUPS OR MEAT JUICES

Home-made stock from real meat and bones or fish still gives the best flavour to foods, often without as much salt as commercial stock preparations. For best results, remove the fat from the stock before using it in cooking or for soups or gravies. This is not difficult.

If you want to use the liquid immediately, pour off any thick layer of fat that has formed on the surface, taking care not to pour off the juice underneath, then lay pieces of paper towel, one at a time, flat on the surface of the liquid. The paper will soak up the fat on the top in preference to the water-based liquid. Carefully lift off the paper towel and discard it, then repeat the process with a clean piece if fat still remains. When you can see the shimmer of only a few tiny globules on the surface, most of the fat has gone.

If you do not need the liquid straight away, the easiest way to remove the fat is to place it in the fridge overnight in a jug or bowl. In the morning, the fat will have solidified on the top and can usually be removed in one piece. With chicken stock, the fat may be soft on top of a jellied stock. In this case, scrape off the fat carefully with a knife or spoon.

FAT-REDUCED GRAVY

Despite much advice to cut down our animal fat intake, there is still nothing like a sizzling roast with gravy made from the juices.

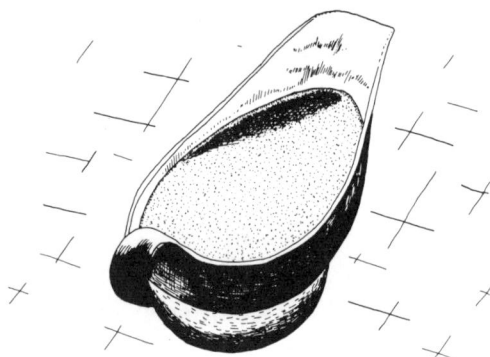

If you are concerned about your cholesterol intake, you can still have your gravy without the same amount of fat by using this simple technique:
• While your roast is cooking, make a thin paste with a tablespoon or two of cornflour (depending on how much gravy you are making and how thick you like it) and water, then thin it with a little more water. Cook it until thick, either on a slow heat on the stove (in a non-stick pan) or in 1-minute bursts in the microwave, stirring in between. Leave it aside, covered, until you need it.
• When the meat is cooked, strain off as much fat as you can from the pan juices (see *Removing the fat from stocks or meat juices*) and stir the juices well into the prepared gravy base. If you prefer, you can add the base to the pan, stirring well

over a low heat to mix in the juices which have cooked onto the surface. If necessary, reheat the gravy in a saucepan or in the microwave before serving.

LOW-FAT CHICKEN DISHES

You may well have heard that chicken is lower in fat than red meat and thus better if you are trying to reduce your cholesterol level. This is true provided you eat only the lean meat. Chicken skin is very fatty and will contribute a considerable amount of cholesterol to your diet. For a healthier chicken dish, remove the skin and all visible fat before cooking it. If you feel that this spoils the chicken, try this different way of cooking it.

Make up a marinade of your own or from 1 tablespoon of chopped fresh or commercially-prepared ginger, 1–2 chopped cloves of garlic, 1 tablespoon of honey, 1 tablespoon of soy sauce and 2 tablespoons of Chinese oyster sauce. Marinate the chicken in this, either whole or in pieces, for an hour or two or overnight if you prefer.

Wrap the chicken or the individual pieces in foil, spooning the marinade over the meat before sealing up the parcels. Put the parcel or parcels into a non-stick baking dish and cook the meat in a fairly hot oven (about 200°C) for an hour and then at about 150°C for at least another 30 minutes. (A large whole chicken will need at least two hours.)

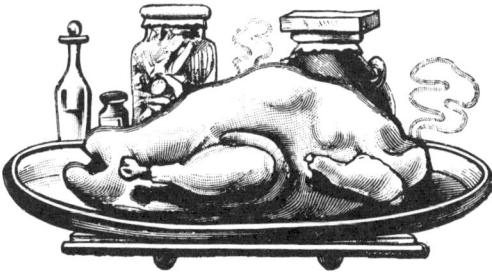

POISONS IN YOUR KITCHEN

The kitchen is never a good place to store poisonous substances but many of us do it out of need or just convenience. If you do store poisons in your kitchen, you need to be aware of the hazard you are creating.

COMMON POISONS AND YOUR CHILD

While most household substances that children might swallow only make them ill for a while, some are potentially lethal. These are:

• PESTICIDES: Both those for household and for garden use are dangerous. These are usually very concentrated chemicals (especially the garden types) and can kill in small amounts. Even camphor blocks and mothballs are dangerous.

• CORROSIVE SUBSTANCES: These strongly acid or alkaline substances burn the digestive tract as they are swallowed. The worst household corrosives tend to be dishwasher detergent, drain cleaner and solder flux. Some pool chemicals, solvents and hobby materials are also strongly corrosive. While you may not routinely store outdoor or hobby materials in the kitchen, you may occasionally mix them up or use and leave them there.

• MEDICATIONS: All prescription drugs, pharmaceuticals and concentrated herbal substances such as volatile herbal oils should be kept away from children. You may think of herbal medicines as mild but this is not necessarily the case. For example, one teaspoon of eucalyptus oil can send a toddler into severe convulsions.

• ALCOHOL: This is also a very dangerous substance to a small child. Compared to what is a normally safe adult quantity, only a little is needed to produce quite a drastic response in a small child. When children gain access to your drink cupboard, they are likely to find some of the stronger varieties, especially if they are sweet, like liqueurs or fortified wines, the most palatable.

PREVENTING POISONING

There are some simple rules which will help you avoid this problem but they need to be practised conscientiously. If you are generally careful but just once take a risk, this could be the time your toddler takes a chance too.

It is easy to be careful when everything is running smoothly. The time the accident happens will probably be when the baby (or your mother or the older child or even the dog) has been sick all night and you've been up and down nursing them. You collapse, exhausted, at 5.30 am to get a little sleep while you can, and leave everything to be tidied up in the morning. The toddler gets up half an hour earlier than usual and eats the rest of the medicine you have left on the kitchen bench from the night before.

To make your system foolproof — or as foolproof as systems can ever be in a home — you need to train yourself and the rest of the family to do these things as a matter of habit:

• Lock all medicines, pesticides, corrosives and any other dangerous substances in a cupboard with a child-resistant catch (you can buy these from hardware stores) or, better still, a key-operated lock. If you do have a lock, never leave the key in it or within the child's reach. Preferably, keep it somewhere the child does not know. Children love a challenge and learn easily.

• Never store dangerous substances in empty food or drink containers. Even with the correct label on, they could be consumed mistakenly by adults or older children. Those most at risk, children under three years old, normally can't read the label but may recognise the container as belonging to something they like. Apart from the danger to children, if you re-use the container for food or drink afterwards, there is a risk that traces of the poison might remain inside, especially inside the lid, and contaminate the food.

• Having dangerous products in containers with child-resistant tops can help, but does not guarantee safety. Children often learn to open child-resistant tops. To a bright and strong child, they can present a challenge.

• Keep monitoring your child's development. This is the most rapid time of children's growth and they become more competent week by week. What they couldn't open or reach last week, they probably can this week.

• If you can't find a way to lock a cupboard or drawer which contains sharp knives, dangerous tools or poisonous materials, it is best to find another place to store them.

• A temporary fastener for some cupboard doors can be made with a strong elastic band or a pony-tail fastener. (Bear in mind that many inquisitive toddlers will learn to solve this puzzle after a few tries.) If the doors on your cupboard meet in the middle, fasten the band over the pair of knobs, holding them together. When you want to open the door yourself, it is just a matter of moving the band onto one of the knobs, to be replaced as soon as you have finished.

• If there is a toddler in the house, never just put something dangerous down for a minute while you answer the phone or the door or attend to something else. If you are usually careful, something the child cannot normally touch may have added attractiveness.

• Spring-clean your medicine cupboard at least once a year and throw away out-of-date medicines or medicines which are no longer being used. It is not a good idea to keep them 'just in case'. Apart from the fact that they do not keep indefinitely and may not work when you next take them, it is important not to give a medicine prescribed for one person to another. It might not be suitable for them. Simply having them around increases the risk that they might fall into a child's hands.

• Take care when you take the child to the home of someone who does not have a small child, especially grandparents or older people who might have medications close by for convenience. Other people's houses are not usually child-proofed and all sorts of dangerous things might be within reach. When in someone else's house, keep your child in sight at all times.

If you see something dangerous on a coffee table or within reach, it is best to ask politely if it can be moved. Don't assume that you will be able to remove it from the child's grasp if it should be picked up. Even if you are looking at the child at that particular moment, and not at your cup of tea, your host, or something at the window, the child's hand-to-mouth speed may well be faster than your speed across the room.

IF YOU SUSPECT YOUR CHILD HAS SWALLOWED SOMETHING

The first thing to do if you suspect your child has swallowed anything dangerous is to get medical advice immediately. Make sure the telephone number of your nearest health service is kept by the phone. Many public health authorities have a 24-hour poisons advice number. Never try to deal with the problem without proper advice. You might make it worse. There are, however, a few important rules:

• The first rule, as the Hitch-hiker says, is 'Don't panic'. You can do more for your child if you are calm and competent than if you are flustered and ham-fisted. Panic also frightens the child, which might make matters worse. Practise being calm and

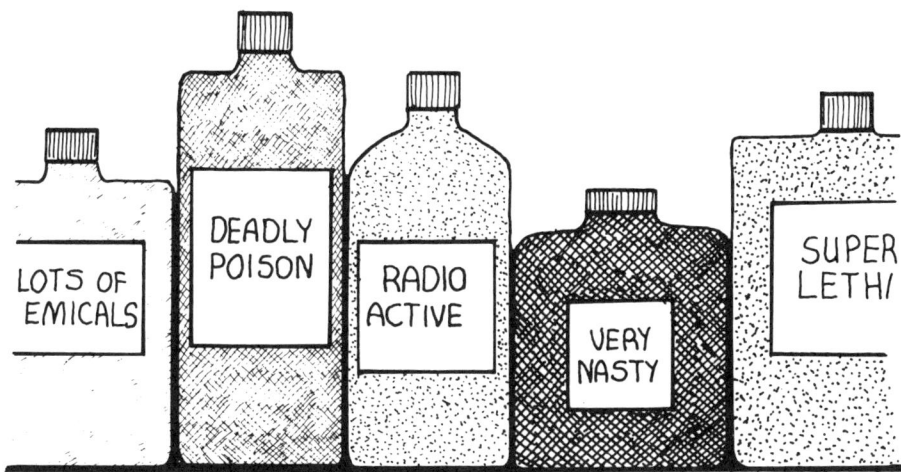

breathing deeply. Count to ten (or more!) if you have to.

• Always ring the doctor or the poisons advice number first, to find out what to do. They will be able to tell you if the amount and kind of poison is dangerous or not. Sometimes the child's reaction may be unpleasant but only transitory. On the other hand, he or she may need urgent treatment. Try to estimate how much of the substance the child has had. This often means knowing what was in the various bottles before, so you have an idea how much is missing.

• Never induce vomiting when a child has taken corrosive poison. This just burns the digestive tract all over again as the poison comes up.

• If the child is not vomiting or going into convulsions AND on advice from the doctor or poisons advice centre, you can give a few sips of milk or water, to help dilute the poison, but never large amounts.

• Never give anything to drink if the child appears to be losing, or may be about to lose, consciousness, after taking sleeping pills, for instance.

• Never give a dose of acid to neutralise alkaline poisons (or vice versa). This only gives a second lot of burns on the way down and does further damage.

• If you have small children and live more than 15 minutes from a hospital or doctor, try to buy a poisons kit from the chemist. These usually contain a bottle of Ipecac syrup and some activated charcoal. This is only a precaution, for very serious cases of poisoning, and is there, if needed, should your doctor or the poisons advice centre tell you to give one of these treatments. (Each is only for certain types of poison.) This may give you more time to get proper help before the child suffers serious harm. Never use them without first being advised by a medical authority and then,

strictly in the amount and manner prescribed.

• If it is an object, rather than a poison, which the child has swallowed, still ring the doctor. Objects which are sharp may do considerable harm and you should take the child to hospital or to a doctor's surgery as soon as possible.

• If the child has an object lodged in his or her throat which is obstructing breathing, hold the child upside down and give a sharp slap on the back. If this doesn't dislodge the object, seek medical help urgently.

POISONS AND THE ENVIRONMENT

Until recent times, most of us would have considered the use of noxious substances only from the point of view of our own immediate health. Now we are conscious of the much wider implications, particularly for our children's health, of what we put into the environment. Although each person's contribution to fighting global pollution may be small, taken together they can make the difference between the survival of a healthy planet and its irreparable damage. By protecting our own local environment, our waterways and our land from dangerous waste, we can help to ensure that our children's future is healthy and, looking further ahead, that our grandchildren have a future.

First of all, most people are now aware, perhaps for the first time, that what goes out of the house on the garbage truck or through the sewerage system does not just disappear, but ends up out there, somewhere. It tends, in fact, to accumulate in huge stockpiles, everyone's unwanted waste, including, amongst the packaging and the debris, a cocktail of poisons, pills and pollution which we would rather not have at home, thank you.

While much of this is harmless, if bulky, dangerous material filters into the environment and ends up, usually, in the soil or the water supply. If it does not harm us directly, it certainly doesn't do too much good for the wildlife and the problem of simply finding space for it is becoming more and more difficult.

POISONS AND OUR WATER

Many of our waste products end up in our water, either through the sewerage system or by leaching out of garbage dumps. This might take them into the sea, where we swim, and they can pollute our food; or into our rivers, creeks, dams and reservoirs, where they again contaminate fish and wildlife, farmlands, crops and even our drinking water.

It is easy to blame industry, but much of the waste which ends up in water systems comes from our homes.

Household cleaners and detergents, fats and oils, pesticides, medicines, chemical wastes from household repairs and hobbies all go down our sinks or off to the tip in our garbage, where they can be washed into waterways by the rain. All of these things can be disposed of safely if we just take the trouble to think about them.

CONSERVING WATER

Even water itself is thrown away. If you live in a town with water laid on you might think that there is an endless supply. In drought-prone countries, however, people remember each summer, when water restrictions may be applied, the precious nature of this resource. Those living in rural areas, with only tank water, or those living in the increasing numbers of communities where water is paid for from the first litre have never doubted it.

We cannot live without water — we will always need to collect it and purify it. Therefore using it without economy can never be justified.

MAINTAINING THE WATER SUPPLY

There are many things you can do to conserve water:
• Install aerators on your taps. These use from two to five times less water, so as well as conserving water, they can save you money on excess water rates and water heating costs.
• Replace leaky washers and repair taps, toilet cisterns or hoses which drip. It is amazing how much water these use.
• Don't run your washing machine or dishwasher with less than three-quarters of a load.
• Encourage the family to wear outer garments a little longer between washes.
• Use a plug and fill the sink when washing dishes rather than washing them under running water. You use less overall.

AVOIDING WATER POLLUTION

• Never pour any type of oil down the sink or the drain. Cooking oil should be poured into an empty can or bottle and sealed before being put into the garbage.
• Use only as much detergent or cleaning agent as absolutely necessary and, where possible, choose bio-degradable varieties.

DISPOSING OF HOUSEHOLD POISONS AND POLLUTANTS

• Buy dangerous products such as chemicals and pesticides in small quantities, so that there is likely to be less waste.
• Always read and follow the instructions on the label when you use or clean up dangerous household chemicals such as pesticides.
• Use rubber gloves to handle any dangerous substance.
• Never rinse out empty pesticide or chemical containers down the sink or

drain. Plastic bags should be wrapped in newspaper and then sealed inside another plastic bag. Other containers should be rinsed out with water three times and the water tipped into a container. This diluted mixture can go over the garden unless it is a herbicide, in which case you should contact your local government authority for advice on where you can take it. Alternatively, leave the container unrinsed ands dispose of it as below:

• NEVER leave chemical containers on the side of the road to await collection.
• NEVER burn chemical containers or aerosols.
• NEVER puncture aerosol cans (of any kind — they can explode).
• NEVER deliver chemical bottles to glass recycling centres.
• NEVER pour surplus chemicals down the sink or drain.
• NEVER re-use chemical containers to store food or drink.
• NEVER dispose of excess chemical concentrates in the garden.

CONSERVING THE WORLD'S RESOURCES

The air and water are not, of course, the only resources we should consider if we are interested in maintaining a healthy lifestyle. Non-renewable resources of all kinds need to be conserved if we are to have adequate food supplies, materials for housing, products we enjoy, and recreational opportunities in the future.

One of the most important things that you can do to help is exercise your rights as a consumer and choose products which do not harm the environment, either in their manufacture, use or disposal. You can also be more sparing with consumable items you use in your own home — this will also bring a cost saving. Here are some suggestions for things you can do in the home to help:

• Buy unbleached or recycled paper products wherever possible to reduce the pressure on our timber resources and the damage to the environment caused by some paper-making processes.
• Use non-disposable instead of disposable products wherever possible, such as crockery, serviettes and so on.
• If your local government authority or other local organisations offer facilities to collect recyclable materials, use these services. In many places you can find people to take motor oil, plastics, batteries and even electrical appliances for recycling. This information is often available from your local government authority.
• Where possible, buy in bulk to reduce the packaging you buy. The packaging costs are added onto the price anyway.
• Take your own basket to the supermarket, rather than using new plastic bags each time, or use the cardboard boxes supplied. These can also be returned or recycled after use.
• Reduce the problem of disposing of packaging materials by choosing products which are not overpackaged or are packed in recyclable or bio-degradable containers, if possible.
• Buy products with an official 'environment-friendly' label if they are available.

DAIRY FOOD AND EGGS

BUTTER

STOP BUTTER BURNING

Many foods taste better sautéed in butter at the start of cooking but the butter burns easily, spoiling the flavour. To prevent butter burning, use half and half butter and oil in the pan and heat them together moderately slowly. Put in the ingredients to be sautéed before the fat gets hot enough to smoke.

NOT ENOUGH FOR YOUR SANDWICHES?

You can extend butter for sandwiches by beating in some fresh milk at the rate of up to 100 mls per 150 g of butter. This not only makes the butter go further but can help to reduce the proportion of animal fat in your diet.

Put your butter in a blender or food processor. (If it is very hard, soften it first for 5 seconds in the microwave.) Turn on the motor with the top lid or feeder open. Pour in the milk in a thin stream through the top opening as the machine is working. Watch the mixture carefully and turn off at the first sign of curdling.

CLARIFYING BUTTER

Clarified butter (ghee) is called for in lots of recipes and has an advantage over normal butter in that it doesn't burn.

To clarify butter, melt the required amount slowly until it stops bubbling (indicating that its water content has evaporated). Let it stand, off the heat, until the sediment settles to the bottom and then pour the clarified butter carefully off the top. The butter which remains, with the sediment, can be used to baste meat or fish for added flavour.

CHEESE IS TASTIER AT ROOM TEMPERATURE

Most cheese is not at its best straight from the refrigerator. Hard cheeses, like cheddar, can be hard to cut and lacking in taste, while soft cheeses may refuse to spread, and Camemberts and Bries can be positively rubbery. To serve cheese at room temperature requires planning and you may not always know ahead of time that you will need it.

This is easily solved with your microwave. Take the cheese out of any foil wrappers and put it on a microwave-safe serving dish. Warm it for 10–20 seconds on Medium and check it. If necessary, give it a little longer. Camemberts will run delightfully, soft cheeses will spread and all cheeses will taste much fuller.

Cream cheeses can also be warmed in this way for up to a minute before mixing them into dips or spreads. They will mix much more easily with the other ingredients.

STALE CHEDDAR CHEESE

Cheddar cheese dries out easily and becomes unpalatable for normal eating. It is still useful in cooking however, especially as a low-cost substitute for Italian cheeses (Parmesan, Pecorino or Romano) over pasta or baked dishes. Allow it to dry completely and cut off any mould. Grate it finely or put it into a food processor or blender and process it into a fine meal. Store it in the refrigerator in an airtight container.

MOULDY CHEESE

If your cheese shows a strong desire to change to a more exotic, blue variety, this need not be a problem. Generally, this is a harmless mould anyway and can be eaten. But if you prefer your cheese in its original condition, simply trim away the surface mould and wipe the cheese over with a clean cloth soaked in a strong salt solution. Allow the surface to dry out at room temperature a little before putting it back in a clean container and returning it to the refrigerator. The salt inhibits the growth of the mould.

If you want to store cheese unopened for a long time, dip it into melted candle wax (or pour the wax over it) ensuring a complete seal. The cheese can be stored in the pantry for weeks if necessary.

EGGS

Storing Egg Yolks

Many dishes call for only a part of the egg to be used — either the white or the yolk. This can be a nuisance if you don't want to use the other part immediately. Egg yolks can be kept in a bowl of water in the refrigerator for a few days until you can find a use for them.

If the membrane has been broken, put them in a small container and carefully pat a piece of cling wrap onto the surface, squeezing out the air. Put on a lid as well and store them in the refrigerator for a few days.

Whites in the Freezer

Egg whites can be frozen in covered containers. Covering the whites is especially important in frost-free freezers, as otherwise they tend to dehydrate. Be sure to label the container with the date and the number of whites it contains as it can be difficult to judge this later on.

Eggs — Fresh or Not?

Today, with modern farming and storage methods, it is unusual for bad eggs to find their way into the shops. But if you keep them a long time or obtain them from an

uncertain source, you may not always be sure they are still fresh enough to use. Once you add a bad egg to a dish, the dish is ruined and you have to start all over again with new ingredients, so it is worth being sure. Here are some simple ways to test an egg for freshness:

• Shake it next to your ear. If you can hear it rattling, it is not fresh.

• Drop it into a basin of cold water at least double the depth of the egg. It is freshest if it sinks straight to the bottom on its side. If it hangs on its end but is still under the water, it is stale but still usable. If it floats at the surface, it is bad and should not be used.

• Hold it up to the light and check the size of the space at the end. If it is bad, additional gases will have collected in the end space. The smaller the air space, the fresher the egg.

• As a final test, always break eggs, one at a time, into a cup before adding them to your recipe. You will know immediately by the smell if they are bad and can throw them away before they spoil the dish. Put each good egg into your recipe mixture or into another dish before you break the next into the test cup.

Storing Whole Eggs

We are all familiar with the fact that eggs are delicate items. We handle them carefully so as not to crack the shell or break the membrane around the yolk. But this is not the end of the story. They are also porous and can absorb smells in the refrigerator from anything strong, like cheese, fish or onion. Place them away from such items, or keep strong-smelling foods in sealed containers or bags.

Eggs keep for a long time in the refrigerator, but their keeping time can be lengthened by wiping them over with vaseline or cooking oil. This blocks up the pores and prevents air getting in.

Dark rings around egg yolks

To hard-boil eggs for a cold dish without getting a dark ring around the yolk, crack the shells slightly as soon as they are cooked and immediately plunge them into cold water to cool. This will also make it easier to remove the shells when they are cold.

Egg filling for sandwiches

Egg sandwiches are nutritious and are especially popular with children. Once cooked eggs cool, the white becomes harder and can be difficult to combine successfully with the yolk. By mashing them with a little butter or yoghurt and some seasonings while they are still warm, a good spreadable mixture that makes an excellent sandwich filling is formed. Half a teaspoon of parmesan cheese per egg in the mixture brings out the eggy taste. Chill it in the refrigerator before using.

Hard-boiled eggs without cracks

Do you suffer from anxieties at the thought of boiling eggs? Do you ever watch miserably as the contents bubble out into the water, making a mess of both egg and pan?

Eggs crack because the contents expand more than the shell and force their way through. The only sure way to prevent this is to provide an escape route for some of the contents. Conveniently enough, each egg contains a small air space in the big end. By pricking the shell at this end, you allow the expanding egg to push the air out and so make more space for itself inside. Use a pin with a big head (for grip) or, if you eat a lot of hard-boiled eggs, buy a special egg-pricker in a kitchen shop. Give the egg a sharp, shallow prick just into the shell at the big end (just far enough in to avoid breaking the membrane around the white itself) and then put it straight into the pan.

If you prefer, you can reduce the tendency of the shells to crack by putting some pieces of cut lemon or some vinegar into the water. This is less reliable but will inhibit the insides from boiling out if they do crack. Heating them from cold, rather than plunging them into hot water, also helps.

If you haven't pricked your eggs and need to salvage the situation when they do crack, you can reduce the amount of egg which boils out by quickly adding a tablespoon of salt or a dash of vinegar or lemon and turning the heat down to a simmer, rather than a vigorous boil. If they are cooked on too high a heat, they will tend to be tough anyway.

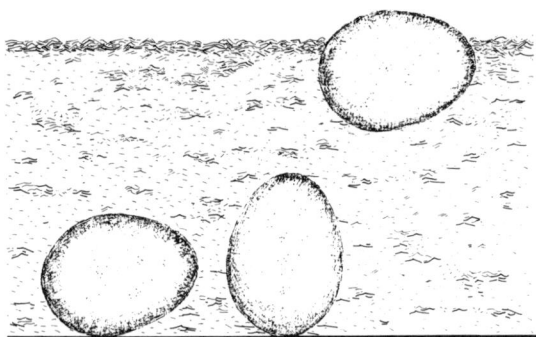

Keep the yolks in the centre

If you want to use hard-boiled eggs for garnishing or for stuffing, it can be a lucky dip when you cut them, to find out whether the yolks have cooked neatly in the centre or have jammed themselves hard up against the side of the shell. This is very annoying when you want them to look neat or to stuff them without breaking the whites. To keep the yolk in the centre, put the eggs in cold water and bring them to the boil, stirring constantly until they are boiling well. This prevents the yolk settling at the side of the shell.

Peeling hard-boiled eggs

It is sometimes frustratingly difficult to peel hard-boiled eggs without taking off a layer of the white. Not only is this wasteful, but if you are planning to serve them in an attractive way, it certainly spoils the appearance. Really fresh eggs are the most difficult to peel and sometimes the problem can be helped just by keeping eggs for a few days before boiling them. You can also make them easier to peel by lightly cracking them and putting them into cold water as soon as they come out of the pan. This will also prevent the dark rings forming around the yolks.

Cutting hard-boiled eggs

Do your egg yolks cake onto the knife when you try to halve or slice hard-boiled eggs? A way to prevent this is to rinse the knife blade in hot water and wipe it dry immediately before cutting. If you have to cut a lot of eggs or slices, repeat the treatment every few cuts, as the blade begins to grab the yolks again.

STUFFING EGGS

Stuffed eggs are a delicious and attractive item for salads and entrées. Put the egg in a bowl of cold water to cool it quickly and do not cut it in half until it is quite cold. Once you have removed the yolk to mix with the other stuffing ingredients, return the whites to the cold water (preferably in the refrigerator) while you mix the filling. This keeps them cool and firm and makes them easier to fill without breaking.

POACHING EGGS

These days, poached eggs are most often cooked in little poaching pans, so that disintegration of the egg isn't a problem. However, if you prefer to poach yours the traditional way, floating in a pan of water, they are still likely to disintegrate as they cook. You can stop this by introducing a little acid, in the form of lemon juice or vinegar, into the poaching water. The eggs will stay whole and firm.

NO WASTE EGG IDEAS

Do you hate waste in the kitchen? Do you avoid using recipes which only call for whites or yolks of eggs because you don't like to waste the other part? Have you ever wondered whether there is something constructive you can do with egg shells? Here are some ideas:

• When you use the whites of eggs for a dish, drop the yolks, one at a time, into boiling water and hard-boil them. Alternatively, prick the membrane and microwave them in individual small dishes on High for half a minute or so, until they are firm (but not hard!). Store them in an airtight container in the refrigerator and use them, grated or finely sliced with a potato peeler, to decorate savoury dishes. They are good over white sauces, on rice, on salads and on many other dishes.

• If you don't want to eat the yolks because of their cholesterol content, they make a good hair rinse, as long as you use lukewarm rather than hot water. (Hot water will cook the egg and you will be picking out strands of cooked yolk for some time!)

• Store fresh egg yolks covered with a little water in a sealed refrigerator container for up to a week. They store best if they are unbroken.

• Unused egg whites can be stored in the freezer in a covered container. You will need to mark the label with the number of egg whites inside and the date.

• Egg shells can be used to clarify soups or coffee by adding them, crushed, to the fluid and boiling gently for five minutes. Then strain the shells from the liquid for a really clear result.

• Scatter crushed egg shells onto your garden (except around azaleas, proteas or other acid-loving plants) as the lime in them sweetens the soil.

PROOFING AN OMELETTE PAN

Perfect omelettes are not difficult to make. The main secret is in the pan. A shallow pan which does not stick is important. An aluminium, cast iron or stainless steel pan can be made non-stick for omelettes by

proving it with oil and salt first (see elsewhere in this book). Don't wash up your omelette pan after use. Simply wipe it out with a moist cloth and no detergent.

SEPARATING EGGS

As any cook eventually finds out, if the smallest amount of yolk gets into the egg white, it will not whisk up properly. This is because of the fat in the yolk. The same will apply if the bowl or utensils you use are greasy.

If you dread separating eggs because all too often the yolk shows a decided tendency to want to unite with its watery neighbour, you might find it worthwhile to buy an egg separator from a kitchen shop. If you are determined to master it without such an aid, there are easier ways:

• Eggs separate more easily when they are cold, although to beat the white, you will get better results if you let it warm to room temperature first.

• Fresh eggs can separate easily if you break them gently into a saucer and then stand a glass upside down over the yolk. Holding the glass gently against the saucer, tip the white into a bowl. The yolk should stay, unharmed, in the glass.

THICKENING MIXTURES WITH EGG YOLK

Nothing beats the flavour of custards and sauces thickened with egg yolk. Nothing is as frustrating as curdling the mixture, just as you were preparing yourself for a culinary triumph. Excess heat, too quickly, is the main culprit in curdling egg yolk sauces. To be safe, always add the egg yolks to the mixture off the heat and stir very well. If you have a double boiler, use this to heat the mixture gradually over water. If you don't have one, you can put a suitable sized bowl or small saucepan in a larger one containing water to get the same effect (see *Claytons Double Boiler*). You can also increase your chances of success by adding a tablespoon of cornflour (dissolved into a paste) to the mixture before cooking it. When returning the mixture to the stove, stir it constantly and make sure it does not come back to the boil.

If the sauce does start to curdle, immediately remove it from the heat. Whisk it thoroughly by hand or with a portable beater until it starts to combine again. Alternatively, pour it into a blender or food processor and blend it on high speed for a minute or so. Heat it very gently after this and do not let it boil. Stir it constantly while it is on the heat.

WELL-WHISKED EGGS

Really fresh eggs do not beat very stiffly. You will get the best results if they are a day or two old. When whisking egg whites, there are some hints for improving your results:

• Add a pinch of salt, a little vinegar, or a pinch of cream of tartar to the whites before whisking. They will become fluffier.
• Use them as soon as possible after they are whisked. If you leave them standing for any length of time, they will go back to liquid and will not whisk up again.
• If you are planning to fold them into a mixture, don't whisk them too dry or they will not combine readily with the other ingredients without losing their bulk. Always fold in the other mixtures. Stirring whisked whites will break the air bubbles and make the mixture sink.

EXTEND WHIPPED CREAM

If you want to make whipped cream go further and, at the same time reduce your fat intake, try this idea. For each small bottle of cream you have whipped, whisk one egg white until bulky but still moist. Gently fold this into the cream and you will increase the volume without adding extra fat content.

DON'T WASTE SOUR MILK

In summer, especially, milk can turn sour before you realise it and it may seem a dreadful waste to pour a new carton or bottle down the sink. It needn't be wasted, though, as the bacteria which have turned it sour are the same bacteria you need to make soft cheese. If it is only a small amount, add some fresh milk to make it up to about a litre. Leave it covered on the kitchen bench until it has set — usually only a few hours, especially in warm weather. Then line a colander with a clean piece of sheeting, muslin or cheesecloth and pile in the curdled milk. Gather up the edges and tie them, making a bundle. Hang this over the sink overnight, or over a bowl in the refrigerator, until it stops dripping. (You can use the whey in your soups, casseroles or baking.) Then scrape the cheese into a bowl and flavour it to taste. Try one of these ideas:

• Add chopped fresh or dried herbs and a pinch or two to taste of pepper, chilli, garlic salt, celery salt and/or dried onions.

• Add chopped dried apricots, apples, peel and sultanas, with a tablespoon of Advocaat liqueur, rum or brandy, some nutmeg and a little honey to taste.

MAKING YOGHURT THICKER

Do you make your own yoghurt but find it isn't as thick and smooth as you would like? There are two ways to thicken it:

• You can whisk a proportion of dried milk into your brew when you first add the yoghurt culture to the milk. The amount you use depends on how thick you want your yoghurt so you may need to experiment. Usually ½ cup (60 g) or so per litre is plenty. If you make your yoghurt with all powdered milk, simply increase the quantity of powder without increasing the water. For those who like goats' milk yoghurt, which usually comes out quite thin and runny, goats' milk is also available in powdered form in some health food stores, or you can use the second method, described below.

• The other way is to strain off some of the whey, leaving behind the thicker part of the yoghurt. This generally makes a smoother yoghurt than the powdered milk method. Line a colander with clean cheesecloth (or you can use a piece of cotton sheeting or fine lawn) and set it over a basin. Turn the freshly made yoghurt into this and put it in the refrigerator for about 4 hours. Scrape the thickened yoghurt curd into a canister with a lid and store it in the refrigerator for up to a week. The whey, which contains lots of vitamins and minerals along with a good deal of protein and some milk sugar, can be used in cooking within a day or two or frozen for later use. (Don't worry if you forget to take it out of the refrigerator. If it has set a little too thickly next day, simply stir a little of the whey from the basin underneath back into the curd.)

WAYS WITH WHEY

If you make cheese or thickened yoghurt at home, you will probably end up with quantities of whey which you don't know what to do with. It is a shame to throw it down the sink as it contains nearly half the protein of whole milk and lots of the vitamins and minerals. It used to be fed to the pigs to fatten them because it is such a nutritious food. Its mildly acid taste is caused by the harmless bacteria which sour the milk.

You can store your whey in a covered jug in the refrigerator, but only for a few days — it becomes progressively more acid. If you don't want to use it straight away, it freezes well.

Whey can be used in many recipes in place of all or some of the liquid. It has a mildly cheesy taste. Try it in:

• *scones* • *cakes* • *bread and buns*
• *pastry* • *mashed potato* • *soups*
• *stocks and broths* • *stews* • *fruit drinks*
• *rice* • *sauces* • *croquettes and rissoles*

FISH FROLICS

PREPARING RAW FISH

BONING (FILLETING) A FISH

It is generally better to fillet a fish before it is cooked.

• Cut off the tail fins with scissors and then cut off the head with a sharp knife, just behind the gills.

• Keeping a sharp, pointed knife close to the bone, slit the fish down the backbone, feeling the rippling of the bone against the knife blade to be sure you are cutting close to the bone. You may need to use short strokes to pare the flesh away from the bone. Lift off the fillet.

• On a big or flat fish, it may be easier to cut only into the centre of the fish, then come back and cut away the other side of the fillet.

• Now turn the fish over and repeat the process to leave the backbone free of the fish.

• If the fish is already cooked, simply ease the knife between the flesh and the bone and lift the flesh off with a fish slice. Lift out the bone and the other fillet is exposed.

SKINNING A FISH

Fillets of fish are much more attractive to look at and to eat without the skins. Unskinned fillets served in a sauce become very messy as people try to remove the skins. The skin is usually

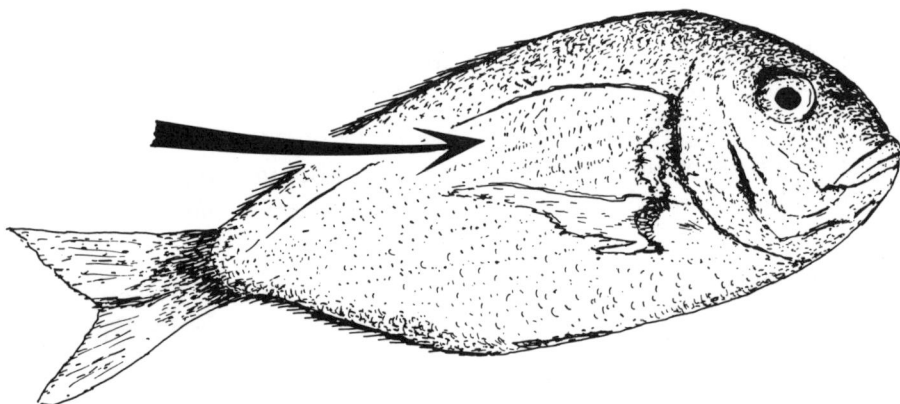

unpalatable, containing strongly-flavoured oils, and will not improve the dish. Moreover, it increases the amount of fishy odour produced during cooking, so removing it will cut down on the residual smell.

Skinning is easier after the fillets are removed. Lay the fillet on a cutting board, skin side down. Gradually work the blade of a sharp, straight-edged knife between the skin and the flesh at the tail end. Then, keeping the knife still as an anchor for the skin, pull the flesh off in a sheet with the other hand, wriggling it back and forth as you lift it off. Alternatively, lay the fish skin side up and pull the skin off the flesh, using the same technique.

To skin flat fish, you need to cut off the fringe of fine fins first with sharp kitchen scissors. Then proceed as above.

NEATER FISH FILLETS

Have you ever wondered why fish fillets served in a restaurant always seem thicker and juicier than the ones you have at home? While some fillets are actually thick, even long, thin ones can be made to seem short and thick with the right preparation technique. You can easily prepare your fish the same way at home for a more professional finish to your fish dishes:

• First, 'bat' the skinned fillets. Place them between two thicknesses of waxed paper or plastic freezer sheets, skinned side down. Using the bottom of a small frying pan or a heavy, flat chopper, 'bat' (slap) the fillets once or twice until they spread about ½ cm wider. This breaks the fibres and prevents them shrinking during cooking.

• Fold the fillet over lengthwise (still skinned-side down), in half if it is not too long, or in thirds if it is very long (tail inside). This gives a more compact and regular shape. If all the fillets are folded to

much the same length (regardless of their length stretched out) they will look more attractive and be easier to organise in the cooking pan. Cooked in the microwave, they are less likely to overcook on the thin portions because the thickness is more even.

VAN DYCK FISH TAILS

When you are serving whole fish, grilled or baked, for a special meal, they look more attractive if the tails are 'van dycked' (named after the beard shape of a famous Dutch artist). To do this, take a pair of sharp kitchen scissors and cut the end of the tail into an accentuated V-shape, with the point towards the end of the backbone. This makes the tails look much better when the fish is brought to the table.

COOKING FISH

CRUMBING FISH

If you have trouble getting breadcrumbs to stick to fish for frying, try adding a little cooking oil to the egg before beating. This helps the crumbs stick to the surface.

FRYING FISH

Fried fish fillets sometimes have a tendency to go soggy on the bottom as they sit in the pan or on the plate after serving. To avoid this, hold each fillet by both ends as you lower it towards the fat and, at the last minute, twist the fillet as you lower it in. This makes an attractive fillet for serving and prevents the fish cooking with a flat surface up against the pan or other fillets. It also allows better fat circulation and makes the fillets crisper.

Drain fried fish on paper towel for a few minutes before serving, to remove any excess fat.

SUCCULENT GRILLED FISH

Grilling is a very good way to cook the more oily types of fish, like the mackerel family, jewfish, mullet, kingfish and reef fish, as it cooks out much of the oil from the flesh. Drier types of fish, like bream, schnapper, flathead, flounder, whiting, plaice, pearl perch or dory need basting with a little butter or margarine for grilling, or the flesh will be dry when cooked.

To grill a whole, thick fish more evenly, make diagonal scores through the flesh down to the backbone. These allow the heat to penetrate the flesh more quickly and cook the centre before the outside is spoiled.

JUICY FISH, LESS SMELL

One of the most delicious ways to cook a fish is to bake it in its own juice with a minimum of flavouring — perhaps a little freshly chopped ginger, a squeeze of lemon juice and a few finely-chopped spring onions, just to enhance its own flavour a little.

The best way to do this is to wrap it in foil to make a packet and put it on a baking dish. Cook it at 180°C for about 20–30 minutes per kilogram. You can tell the fish is cooked when the flesh will part easily in flakes down to the bone when you lift it with a fork. If it is not cooked when you open the packet, simply close it up again and cook it a little longer.

Alternatively, cook it over hot water in a large steamer or even on the barbecue. You can cook it whole or in fillets or chunks, in one packet or several. The fish will be succulent when cooked and you can pour off the juices, serve them with the fish or keep them in the fridge or freezer to use in other fish dishes.

JUICY FISH, LESS WORK

If you want to enjoy all the flavour of a whole fish without the work of all that scaling and skinning, you can use the foil technique to advantage. You will still need to remove the fish gut and gills and clean out the stomach cavity but you can then wrap the fish in foil without removing the scales. The fish is cooked in the same way as described above. If you want to flavour the flesh, put your herbs or flavourings in the cleaned-out stomach cavity before cooking.

When the fish is cooked, the scales and skin will stick to the foil and can be lifted off with it.

REDUCE FISHY COOKING SMELLS

Fish dishes are particularly prone to wafting their smells through the house and staying there. This is particularly true of shellfish, especially prawns.

You can reduce this by adding a tablespoon of vinegar and a bay leaf to the cooking pot. It will not eliminate the smell but it will make it less potent.

SAUCE FOR WHOLE FISH

When you bake a fish whole, it will usually produce a quantity of juice in the pan or the foil. If this is not oily, it makes a delicious sauce to coat the fish, especially if it has been delicately flavoured with herbs or seasonings before cooking.

(You will need to taste a little to decide if you want to use it.)

First pour off the juices and strain out any bones or solids used in flavouring the fish. Put the fish aside somewhere to keep warm. Mix a tablespoon or two of cornflour with a little cold water to make a thin, smooth paste and stir this into the strained juice. In a microwave oven or small saucepan, heat the sauce, stirring as necessary, until it thickens. Adjust the flavour by adding a touch of salt, lemon juice, pepper or whatever you like. Pour the sauce over the fish and serve it.

OLD-FASHIONED POTTED SHRIMPS

Old-fashioned potted shrimps make a delightful starter to a meal or summer accompaniment to salads, and they will keep for up to a week in the fridge if undisturbed.

They are made with a layer of fat or butter over the top which prevents bacteria spoiling them as long as the seal is not broken. You will need at least as much butter for this dish (by weight) as the shelled prawns themselves. Clarified butter (ghee) is best but if you don't have any, you can clarify your own by melting it in a pan then straining off the clear fat from the sediment which falls to the bottom of the pan.

Cook, shell and rinse some fresh prawns and drain them thoroughly (or buy them in this condition). Pat them dry, if necessary, on some paper towel. Season them lightly with pepper, spices and herbs to suit your taste and sauté them lightly in a little butter. Pack them tightly into ramekins, filling any air spaces with the now-flavoured butter.

Heat more clarified butter to cover the top of each dish with up to ½ cm depth of fat. When the butter has melted, pour it over the top of the dish, making sure that there is no exposed prawn surface. Cover the ramekins with plastic wrap to keep out the smells of other foods and then store them in the fridge.

MICROWAVING FISH

MORE EVEN COOKING

Fish don't normally come in neat shapes which microwave well. They tend to have inconvenient thin bits near the tail which can dry out and darken unattractively as they overcook, while the main part of the fish reaches perfection. This is a particular problem when cooking fillets.

To overcome it, overlap the thin parts in the dish or shield them with small pieces of foil. Cook fish until it is nearly done and allow 5 minutes or so standing time to finish it off. Cooked properly in a microwave, fish can reach heights of succulent perfection difficult to obtain with other methods.

MAKING FISH LOOK APPETISING

Because fish remains juicy in the microwave, some fish fillets are prone to collect coagulated juices around them as they cook. This need not be a problem but if you find it unacceptable, try putting a piece of paper towel under the fish in the dish. This will absorb the juices and they will not cling to the fish. Alternatively, raise the fish on a trivet during cooking.

If your fish fillets look unappealingly pale when they emerge from the microwave, try sprinkling or brushing some colourful toppings on them before cooking. You can use these on their own or in combinations:

chopped spring onions, chives, paprika, nutmeg, mushrooms, chopped parsley, seasoned butter, soy sauce, teriyaki sauce, microwave browning, finely-grated cheese, chopped capsicum, flaked crabmeat, shrimps, chopped olives

CRUSTACEANS

SHELLING PRAWNS

Prawns are easy to shell if you are systematic about it. This method can be used with cooked or raw prawns, hot or cold:

• Hold the prawn by its body, in one hand, with its head towards you. Grasp the head with the other hand and pinch it off, pulling downwards towards the prawn's legs. The first set of legs will come off with it.

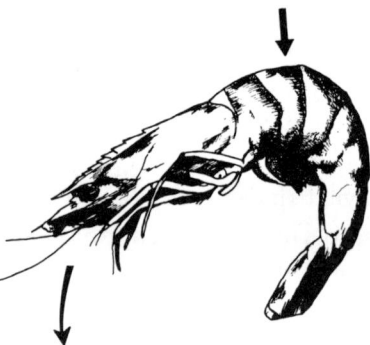

• Now, holding the prawn by the body as before, grasp the next three sets of legs between your free hand and peel them sideways, up and around the prawn's body. This should take with it the shell around the middle part of the body, which will usually come off joined to the legs. Remove any remaining pieces similarly.
• This should leave only one segment of the body shell attached to the tail. Hold the cleaned body in one hand and grasp the tail with the other. Pull the tail down, in line with the body, as though removing a pair of trousers from the prawn.
• Large prawns should then be de-veined (have their stomach thread removed), by running a sharp knife down the middle of the prawn's back, about 2 mm below the surface. This should expose the dark vein, which can then be peeled out with the tip of the knife. Rinse the cleaned prawns in cold water before use.

CLEANING CRABS

You will usually need to kill crabs by cooking them in fresh water or freezing, as they are very difficult to kill in any other way. To clean a cooked crab, lift out the tail flap from the underside of the shell and pull it upwards until the top of the shell breaks away from the rest of the body. Break the body down the centre, from front to back, and remove the buff-coloured, feathery gills. Rinse away all the loose tissue from the inside of the shell, saving and thoroughly rinsing any bright orange flesh, as this is the roe (the eggs) and is good to eat. What remains is good, edible flesh.

To remove the flesh from the claws, break each joint away from its neighbour and carefully pull it away. Sometimes the flesh will simply pull out from the shell, still attached to the next joint. If not, carefully crack open each segment (you can use a nutcracker) and remove the flesh. Discard the soft, clear bone in the centre of each segment.

KILLING LOBSTERS

If you have ever sworn off lobsters after cooking one live and hearing it dying in the pot, try this quicker, quieter method of killing them next time. It is a humane method and has particular advantages if you are planning to microwave or barbeque a lobster rather than boil it or if your boiling pot is not very large.

Choose a strong, sharp, pointed knife. Hold the lobster by the tail with its head away from you, underside down. Firmly push the point of the knife deep into its back through the join between the head section and the first segment of the tail.

This severs the spinal cord and kills the lobster. It may continue to move for a few minutes, but not for long.

Alternatively, you can put the live lobster in the freezer for 30–45 minutes. Then remove it from the freezer and cook it immediately.

KEEP LOBSTERS STRAIGHT WHILE COOKING

Lobsters usually arrive at the table with their tails curved around to meet the underside of their bodies. For decorative purposes, you might sometimes want to serve a lobster stretched out on a platter. For this method, you need to kill your lobster first (if you have bought it live).

To keep its tail straight while cooking, take a wooden skewer at least as long as the tail. Hold the (dead) lobster underside up. Push the sharp end of the skewer into the tail end and slide it along, through the meat, just under the shell, toward the head. This pegs the body straight during cooking and prevents the tail curling around.

For a final touch, slit down the centre of the underside of the shell with a sharp knife and remove the dark thread of the gut. This gives the lobster a more appetising appearance when it is served.

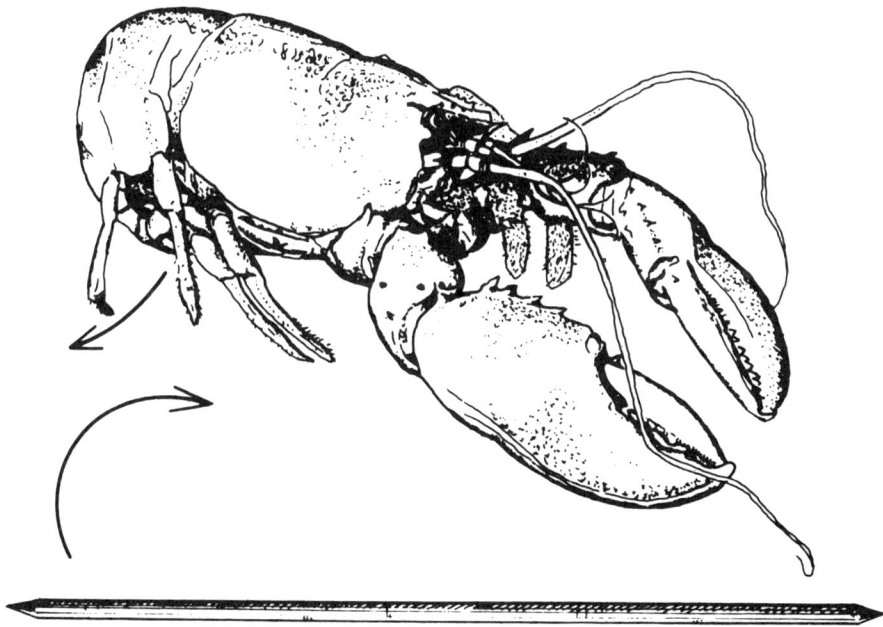

MEAT MAGIC

ROASTS

HOW LONG TO COOK?

Sometimes it is difficult to find a recipe for the actual cut of meat you have bought to roast. If you have cooked it many times before this may not present a problem. However, if you are not used to cooking without a recipe it can be useful to have a rule of thumb to guide you in choosing cooking times and temperatures.

Tender cuts of meat (such as lamb, beef fillet) can be cooked in a medium to hot oven, about 180-190°C. You need to allow about 40–50 minutes per kilogram, with about 20 minutes over, depending on how rare you want the meat to be. This will give a well-browned outside and moist interior, but there will be a fair degree of shrinkage. If you suspect the meat is not as tender as you would like, you are better to use a slow to medium oven, about 165–175°C. You need to allow about an hour per kilogram for rare meat and about 1 ¼ – 1 ½ hours per kilogram for well done. Cooking the meat slowly will result in less shrinkage and a more tender finish.

LARDING A ROAST

If you are roasting a cut of meat which does not have much fat of its own, it may dry out in the cooking unless it is basted very frequently.

You can reduce this problem by larding — threading small pieces of fat through the outer layer of the meat. These melt during cooking and keep the meat basted.

The fat should be firm, dry and white. Pork or bacon fat is best. Cut it into thin strips, about ½ cm wide and 3 cm long, with a knife or kitchen scissors. With a sharp knife, make slits in the meat, cutting in at a shallow angle to keep close to the surface. Poke the strips into the cuts, leaving a tail sticking out of the meat. Alternatively, thread the fat strips, one at a time, onto a poultry needle and sew them, with one stitch each, into the surface, leaving the tails sticking out.

Small, tender roasts, like whole fillets, can be wrapped around entirely with strips of fatty bacon for the same purpose.

This is called Barding. The meat should be roasted on a trivet in a hot oven (about 200°C) after this, to make sure the fat melts and toasts the outside of the meat rather than letting the meat become soggy on the outside. This type of joint will not toughen at high temperatures.

GOLDEN ROAST CHICKEN

For a really deep colour on your roasted chicken, turkey or duck skins, and a delicious flavour, brush a little honey over the skin before putting it in the oven. (If you are cooking a big turkey, it is best not to brush on the honey until the last hour or less of cooking time or it can darken too much.)

A similar result can be obtained by brushing the skin with oil. The colour will also be improved by sprinkling some paprika over it before cooking.

CRACKLING-GOOD PORK

One of the main pleasures of roast pork can be the crackling. When it is crisp, it is delicious. When it is leathery, it can be more than a disappointment — it can be a downright frustrating test of the strength of your jaw. To make the crackling crisp, here are some simple suggestions:
• Get the butcher to score the skin well or use a sharp knife to do it at home. Cuts should be about 1 cm apart and right through the depth of the skin.
• Rub the skin with oil and salt before cooking.
• Use a very hot oven (at least 200°C), either at the beginning or the end of the cooking, for about half an hour. The heat melts the fat out of the skin and fries the top layer crisply as it does so.
• Keep the skin on the top and don't turn the meat over while it is cooking. This ensures that it has the greatest share of the heat and does not have to stew underneath the meat in juices which would soften it.

ROASTING MEAT IN THE MICROWAVE

Which cuts roast best?

Choose the flatter cuts of meat for best results in the microwave. If it is a tougher cut of meat, it will cook better if you simmer it in about 2 cups of water or stock per kilogram for most of the cooking. Strain this off and use it for your gravy when the meat is nearly cooked. For more tender meats, roast uncovered on a trivet, without the water, if you prefer.

Crackling in the microwave

Although microwave ovens do not usually crisp the outside of roast meats, you can make delicious crackling in the microwave.

It is important to score the crackling thoroughly before cooking, as you normally would, and then rub plenty of salt into the skin. When the meat has cooked and is standing, remove the crackling, divide it into portions and put it in a shallow microwave pan with no lid. Microwave it on High for about 4 minutes. It should crisp up very well.

Preparing meat for microwave roasting

Meat roasted in the microwave is often criticised for being rather bland-looking, as it doesn't brown on the surface. If you wish you can improve the finished appearance of the meat by marinating it, or brushing the surface with a commercial browning mixture or shaking some herbs and spices over the top. Paprika is particularly good as it gives a rich colour to the surface. Don't add salt until after cooking — it can toughen the meat.

Microwaved roasts undercooked on the bottom

Sometimes microwave roasts come out underdone on the bottom. Some people like this rare portion, but others prefer the meat to be cooked right through. It happens because the microwaves cannot reach that part of the meat. Microwaves cook by bouncing around the oven and penetrating the food they hit for only about 2–3 cm. A thick joint, sitting on the bottom of the oven, has a large area underneath where the microwaves cannot reach by bouncing or by penetrating from above. That means that this area will only be heated gradually by conduction when the meat next to it is hot.

So if your meat is cooked less on the bottom than you would like, one answer is to elevate it during cooking. This allows the microwaves to bounce up from the floor of the oven and cook the underside. You can raise the meat on a trivet, allowing the fat and juices to drain into the dish underneath during cooking rather than sit around the bottom of the meat. Alternatively, you can sit the whole dish on an upturned microwave bowl or on a stand, to allow plenty of bouncing space.

Another solution is to use a browning dish (preferably a type with a ribbed surface like a built-in trivet) to cook your roasts. They become hot in the microwave oven and hold their heat. This cooks the bottom of the meat.

Cooking method for microwaved roasts

Meat cooked on High power will usually be tough. For best results, cook the meat on Medium power for about 15–30 minutes per kilogram, depending on the tenderness of the cut of meat. For more tender results, especially with tougher cuts, you can turn the power setting to Low for the whole (or for the second half) of the cooking. This will mean increasing the cooking time a little. The meat is done when you can gently part it with a fork.

Microwaved roasts - to cover or not?

Tender cuts of meat do not usually need covering in the microwave. Tougher cuts are better covered with a lid or plastic wrap or put into a roasting bag. This helps to prevent them drying out. However, a complete cover will tend to steam the meat and leave it rather too moist on the surface. There are several solutions to this problem:

• Remove the cover for the last ½ hour to allow the surface to dry out a little and then replace it for the standing time.
• Finish cooking the meat, uncovered, in a hot conventional oven for ½ hour after the standing time.
• Cook the meat by convection/microwave mix, if you have that type of oven.

CARVING MEAT

Nothing can ruin the effect of a beautifully-cooked roast more than hacking it unceremoniously into portions without considering the grain of the meat. Carving is an art but it can easily be learnt and has only a few basic rules:

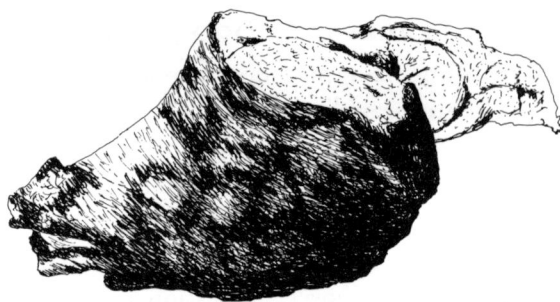

• Allow the meat to rest for up to a quarter of an hour before carving. If you are making gravy from the juices, this should be almost the right amount of time for you to make it. The meat softens and sets a little in this time.
• Always cut across the fibres (the grain) of the meat rather than along them. Cutting along them will result in stringy textured meat. Cutting across the grain will allow you to cut finer slices.
• Put the carving fork into the heart of the meat to keep it from rolling around while you cut. This gives you more control of

the knife. Move the fork as required to keep the meat steady.

• Use long, sweeping strokes rather than a sawing motion. Sawing the meat will give an unattractive ribbed look to the slices. If you have difficulty cutting in long sweeps, your knife is probably not sharp enough.

• When cutting poultry or other meat with a bone, cut towards the bone. You will need to make a cut along the bone (running with the grain) to release each slice from it. Follow the contour of the bone gently with the blade of the knife to slice the meat away without digging into the bone.

• To cut joints of poultry away from the carcass, lift them gently outwards from the body until they start to break at the joints, then carefully cut through the joint to separate it. If you aim only for the general vicinity of the joint with the knife, it can be difficult to find the joint and you can mutilate the meat in that area while looking for it.

• Remove strings from a roast before carving that part of the meat. Cut them with the tip of the knife and peel them off the meat. String should not be served attached to the meat.

• If a cut of meat has small sections enclosed in bone which cannot be sliced where they are, cut that whole piece of meat out in a lump by following the bone with the knife blade. When it is free, sit it on its side on the dish where you can slice it against the grain in the normal way.

• Joints with a bone through the middle, like whole hams, can be carved down to the bone one way and then turned over and carved in similar fashion on the other side.

THE CARVING KNIFE

Never store your good knives in a drawer where they will rattle around with other utensils. This is dangerous if they are sharp and the knives will lose their edge as they grate up against other tools. A wooden knife block or magnetic wall holder will keep the blades apart.

STUFFINGS

BETTER STUFFED MEATS

Many cooks find out to their dismay, when they serve what should have been a feast for the eyes as well as for the mouth, that stuffing usually swells in cooking. A bird or rolled joint which is tightly stuffed will burst somewhere or perhaps distort as the increased volume of filling tries to find a way out.

For stuffed roasts which hold their shape, use only the minimum amount of stuffing to fill the meat and sew or fasten it well before cooking. If you have stuffing mix left over, make a neat pile in the baking dish (or on a baking rack if it is a cut which is likely to produce a lot of fat) and cook it along with the roast. When served, no one will know where it was cooked.

MEAT PREPARATION

THINLY-SLICED MEAT

Today, with the increasing popularity of Asian styles of cooking, many recipes call for meat to be trimmed and sliced very thinly before cooking. This may look very easy when chefs do it on television cookery programs with their beautifully sharpened knives, but when you try it with your normal kitchen knife, the meat is likely to squash about and be difficult to cut thinly enough.

To solve this problem, put the meat in a plastic bag, keeping it flat (on a tray or dish if necessary) and freeze it just a little. The meat should be stiff but not solid. Transfer it to your cutting board and slice it with a very sharp, straight-edged knife. It should slice as thinly as you want it without falling to pieces. By the time you have cut the strips, the meat will be thawed enough to cook straight away.

TENDERISE TOUGH MEAT

Tough meat can be very disappointing — this is not always limited to cheap cuts. On the other hand, some of the cheapest cuts have the best flavour and are, of course, predictably tough. There are many ways to make tough meat more tender:

• Long, slow cooking is the best way to tenderise meat and can reduce the most leathery cut to a melt-in-the-mouth delight. Some meat may need cooking for as much as 6–8 hours at 110–130°C. Crock pots are designed to take advantage of this and produce very good results with this type of meat. Because the food is cooked slowly, the ingredients retain their shape and texture rather than dissolve into a mush. The same results can be obtained by using cast iron pots or pottery casseroles in the oven for a long, slow cook. The long cooking time kills harmful bacteria which can grow in the food if it is cooked at low temperatures for only a short time.

• Pressure cookers are a useful way to speed up the cooking of cuts which would normally need very long cooking. By increasing the temperature at which the food boils, it cooks much faster. However, if overcooked, the ingredients tend not to retain their own identity and can dissolve, instead, into a very tasty thick sauce or soup.

• Marinating meat in a mixture containing acid (like wine, vinegar or fruit juice) will tenderise the meat and add flavour. You can also use Worcestershire sauce or French dressing, taking care not to overdo the flavour. Marinate it for at least an hour or, for really succulent results, overnight.

• Pawpaw contains a natural tenderiser called papain, mainly in its fruit but also a little in its leaves. If you want to cook very tough meat, marinate it in a mixture which contains pawpaw flesh or chopped leaves for an hour or two before cooking and/or cook it with pawpaw. The meat should be much more tender and the flavour will be enhanced. (Unless it is really tough, do not marinate meat too long in pawpaw mixtures or the surface can become too mushy.)

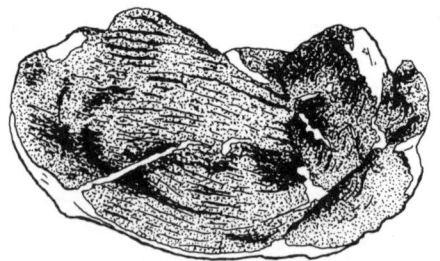

• If you do not have a ready supply of pawpaw, you can buy commercially-prepared papain as a meat tenderiser. Shake this onto the meat before cooking and it will soften the meat as it cooks.

• Pounding the meat with a wooden mallet helps to break down the fibres and is a useful way to tenderise meat which will be cooked quickly without tenderising marinades or sauces.

FLATTENING MEAT

Traditional Viennese and/or Italian veal dishes need veal steaks to be very thin. To prepare the meat for a perfect result, choose a large, straight-edged kitchen knife, preferably with a fairly heavy blade. Lay the meat on a chopping board and systematically beat it with the blunt edge of the knife. This breaks up the fibres and tenderises the meat. Then flatten the meat by beating it a few times with the flat side of the knife.

STOP THE SHRINKS!

Have you ever despaired at seeing the bacon curl in the pan to a convoluted rope or finding your steaks or chops doing contortions in the grill pan? The result is often a checkerboard of burnt and rare meat with a very tough edge where the skin is. This is due to the greater shrinkage at that edge and can be easily prevented by snipping the rind or the skin edge with a sharp knife or a pair of scissors before cooking. The skin will still shrink but it will do so in small sections, preventing the rest of the meat from curling up to follow it.

MEATBALLS THAT STAY WHOLE

Meatballs have a bad habit of falling apart during cooking. The same fate can befall rissoles, especially when the fat content of the meat is high. You can reduce this problem by adding an egg (or an extra one) to the mixture and by dipping each meatball or rissole into water before rolling it in flour. This helps it to collect extra flour and make a firmer coating around the meat.

HAM AND BACON

DRESSING A WHOLE HAM

A whole ham is still part of the Christmas tradition and, in warmer climates, is usually served cold rather than hot. You can dress a ham for the table with a spicy coating which will improve the flavour.

First, skin the ham if it is not already skinned. Take a bunch of parsley which is clean and quite dry. Using a blender (or food processor, if possible), chop it as finely as you can and then sprinkle it over the surface of the ham. Sprinkle over this some very fresh nutmeg — a whole, freshly grated one is best. This mixture will keep well and gives a wonderful warm flavour to the meat.

BOILING A HAM

Ham should be soaked in water overnight to remove excess salt. Next day, throw away the water and use fresh water to cook the meat. To boil the ham, choose a pan with a lid. Put in the ham with enough water to cover it and bring it to the boil. Add some herbs, a little honey and, perhaps, some mustard. When it begins to boil, put on the lid and immediately turn the heat right down to a simmer. Cooking the ham too fast will make it tough. It will normally take about 45–60 minutes per kilogram, depending on the age (and thus the toughness) of the meat.

When the ham cools enough to handle, the skin should be removed by sliding a sharp knife under the edge of it and pulling. It will usually peel off. The

exposed fatty surface of the ham can be decorated with fresh breadcrumbs (sometimes put on over a spreading of beaten egg) and studded with cloves or sprinkled with spices. Roast the dressed ham in an open pan (or the oven grill if you have one) until the dressing turns golden brown.

CRISP BACON FROM THE MICROWAVE

Although the microwave is not noted for producing crisp food, it can produce beautifully crisp bacon without spattering and with less curling and shrinkage.

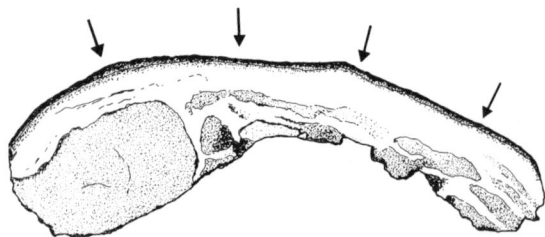

The secret is in the use of paper towel between the layers of bacon as they cook. Arrange the bacon in a row on a sheet of paper towel. Cover it with another sheet and, if you like, with another layer of bacon. You can layer up to about 2 ½ cm thickness in this way, finishing with a layer of paper. Microwave the bacon on High for 4 minutes per layer. Remove the bacon and allow it to stand, without separating the layers, for about 5 minutes to finish cooking. During this time it will become more crisp.

MAKE MINCE GO FURTHER

Budgets have to stretch further and further these days. At the same time, we are hearing a lot about how we should eat more vegetables and grains to increase the fibre in our diets.

You can kill two birds with one stone by using these simple techniques to make minced meat go further in the family meal. Chances are, no-one will realise they are not eating a solid meat dish:

• Make a meat sauce for a bolognese or savoury mince with half-and-half meat and finely grated vegetables and/or pulses (carrot, celery, onion, parsnip, lentils, or any combination of these). Add a good dollop of tomato paste to enrich the flavour and give a good, meaty colour. Simmer the mixture for at least 30 minutes to ensure that the vegetables cook down to a soft texture. Serve as usual with rice, baked potatoes, pasta, toast or whatever you prefer.

• When you make a meatloaf, meatballs or hamburgers, mix the minced meat with about the same amount (by bulk) of quick-cooking rolled oats. Season the mixture well. If you like, you can add chopped onion, tomato paste, herbs, chopped ginger, chilli, Worcestershire sauce or whatever flavouring ingredients you prefer. Add a little water, if necessary, to make the moistness of the mixture about the same as the normal mince-only version, and cook it in the usual way.

VEGETABLES

ARRANGING VEGETABLES IN THE MICROWAVE

You can cook different vegetables together on one dish in the microwave by arranging them so that you take advantage of the oven's tendency to cook more on the outside than on the inside. Prepare your vegetables and arrange them on a plate with the harder, slow-cooking vegetables to the outside and the softer, quick-cooking ones in the middle. Cover them with plastic cling wrap and microwave them. An average family quantity of vegetables (enough for 4 people) usually takes about 7 minutes. Check them from time to time to see if they are done, starting a couple of minutes before you expect them to be ready.

BEANS WITHOUT AN ILL WIND!

Beans and pulses are very good foods, but many people are afraid of them because of their reputation for causing flatulence.

If you want to eat them without the after-effects, try soaking them in fresh water overnight before cooking them. Next day, throw away the soaking water and cook them in fresh water. You will not lose a significant amount of their nutrients and they will be much more appreciated.

CABBAGE SMELLS

Does your house reek of cabbage every time you cook it? This offensive smell is difficult to stop entirely, but a stale crust of bread placed on top of the cabbage while it is boiling will help to absorb the smell.

If you have a microwave, cook the cabbage in a plastic bag (with a teaspoon or two of butter) loosely tied at the neck. When cooked, shake it a little to coat the cabbage with the butter. It tastes delicious and will be much less smelly as it cooks.

AVOCADOS

Buy avocados when they are still firm to touch but don't use them until they start to soften. With soft-skinned avocadoes it is easy to judge when they are ripe, but the thick-skinned type, like Hass, may still feel firm. They are usually ready when the little stub of stalk will easily lift off the end.

Use a sharp knife to cut an avocado around from top to bottom, cutting in as far as the stone all around. The two halves should easily twist apart if it is ripe, leaving the stone in one side. To remove the stone, push the tip of a knife gently into the bottom end of the stone, where it meets the flesh of the avocado, and lever it out. (Do this gently or it will shoot across the kitchen.)

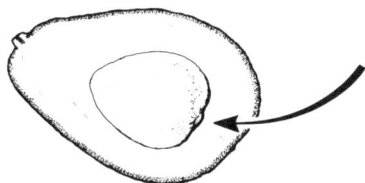

Cut avocados into quarters lengthways if you want to cut them up or use them out of their shells. Hass avocados can be eased out of the shell by running a sharp knife around the edge of it and peeling it back. Soft-skinned avocados can be peeled by lifting the skin at one end with a knife and pulling it away from the flesh. If you are preparing avocados ahead of time, sprinkle a little lemon juice on them to stop them turning brown.

For an attractive decorative effect, skin quarters of avocado and then make long cuts through the flesh as though slicing it, from the thick end to the thin end, stopping just short of the tip. Fan the slices out and use them to decorate salads or seafood.

If you are only using one half of the avocado at a time, leave the stone in position and use the other half, as the flesh keeps better with the stone in place. Cover it tightly in cling wrap, excluding any air. It will keep for a few days in the refrigerator.

Avocado tends to discolour and change its flavour when it is cooked for any length of time, so if you want to cook it, it is best to add it late in the cooking process.

BLANCHING VEGETABLES FOR THE FREEZER

When vegetables are plentiful, especially if you grow your own, you can take advantage of this by freezing them in meal-sized, pre-prepared quantities. Before freezing vegetables, it is important to blanch them to kill any germs (on the skins) which might be dangerous when the food thaws. You can do this by:
• plunging them for a minute or two in boiling water and then draining them, or
• putting them in plastic bags tied loosely at the end and microwaving them on High for a minute or two. Then plunge the bag into cold water, to stop the cooking. When cool, freeze them without opening.

FREEZING TOMATOES

Like so many seasonal fruits and vegetables, tomatoes are very cheap at some times and very expensive at others. You can capitalise on their cheapness by freezing them for cooking later. Wash them and allow them to dry. Then put them, whole, into plastic bags and freeze them (remembering to label and date the bags!). For use, remove them from the freezer and thaw them wholly or partly. The skins will come away easily and should be discarded, leaving the tomatoes ready to put straight into casseroles, soups or stews.

FRESH HERBS FROM YOUR FREEZER

To store fresh herbs without drying them (hence losing some of the flavour), first wash them and shake them dry. Put them into a plastic bag and seal it, then place the bag in the freezer. When you are ready to use the herbs, remove the bag from the freezer, leaving it sealed, and immediately crush the herbs, while still frozen, rubbing the bag briskly between your hands. This has the effect of finely chopping the herbs and separating them from the stalks. The stalks can be removed from the package and the unused portion sealed up and returned to the freezer. This technique works particularly well on the more tender-leafed herbs like basil and mint.

CHOOSING AND STORING HERBS AND SPICES

Always buy dried herbs and spices in small jars or packets as they quickly lose their flavour when opened. They keep best in glass or ceramic containers with tight-fitting lids. If you buy them in cardboard or cellophane packs, it is worth transferring them to corked or lidded jars immediately.

Don't store herbs and spices near the stove or beside a bright window, as light and heat will rob them of their aroma and flavour even more quickly. Ideally, they should be kept in a dark pantry.

Never add fresh herbs or spices to a container which still holds old ones that have lost their flavour because the new ones will then fade faster. If necessary, throw the old stock away. If you buy in small amounts, you should not lose too much.

ONIONS

ONION SMELLS ON YOUR HANDS

Onions have a unique way of leaving their smell behind. Even after washing your hands thoroughly, you may be annoyed to find your hands smelling of onions hours later or even the next day.

To remove the smell, pour a little milk over your hands and rub them thoroughly, then rinse in fresh water. The smell should disappear immediately. For very stubborn smells, rinse your hands well in a diluted bleach solution and then wash them in soap. Rub in a little handcream to prevent

the skin becoming chapped and the smell should be gone.

ONION SMELLS IN THE CHOPPING BOARD

Chopping boards, too, absorb onion smells and some cooks like to have a separate one for onions. If you don't run to such luxuries, you can still manage to have a sweet-smelling board to cut the fruit or the bread after preparing the onions. Simply wipe a little diluted bleach over the board after use (wear rubber gloves if you have them), leave it for a few minutes and then rinse it thoroughly. The smell will be replaced by a clean bleach smell which will disappear as the board dries.

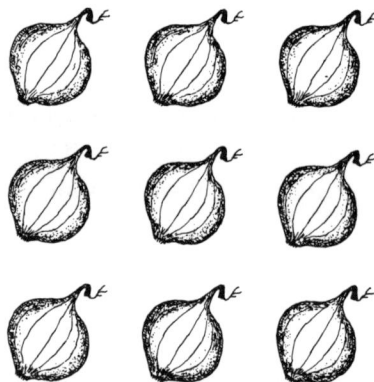

ONIONS - NO MORE TEARS

Onions are delicious but are a cook's nightmare. If you suffer from streaming eyes every time you prepare them, there is a solution. The tears are a result of volatile fumes which rise from the delicate membrane between the fleshy layers of the onion when it is cut or torn. They can be reduced considerably by one of the following methods:

• soak the onions in cold water for half an hour before preparing them, or

• peel them under cold running water, or

• rinse them well under cold running

water after topping and tailing them and before peeling them, or

• peel the dry skin by lifting it with the edge of the knife, avoiding tearing the membranes in the juicy part underneath. Then use a very sharp knife to cut the onion up. The vapour released when the juicy flesh is torn or bruised is what causes the tears, so the trick is to minimise the actions which produce it.

CHOPPING ONIONS EASILY WITHOUT A FOOD PROCESSOR

Peel the onion without cutting off the root end. Cut it from top to bottom into halves. Take each half in turn. Hold it at the root end and make parallel cuts about 1 cm apart (or less) into the onion from the top, with the knife point facing toward the root but stopping just short of it. Then, holding the onion by the root, slice it up as though you are cutting onion rings, across the cuts you have just made. The onion will be neatly chopped.

PULSES

SOFTER PULSES

Beans and peas will be softer if they are cooked in water without added salt. So, too, will cabbage. If you want to cook them to tender perfection, do not add any salt until after they are done.

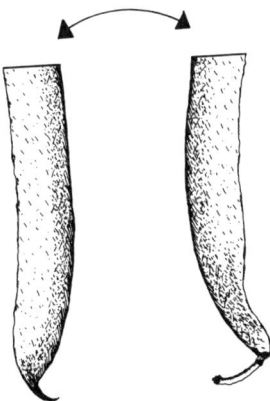

POTATOES

CRISPER MICROWAVED POTATOES

If you love to cook potatoes whole in their jackets in the microwave but are disappointed that the skins often come out rather soft, try putting a layer or two of paper towel under the potatoes as they cook. This absorbs a lot of the moisture and the potatoes will come out dryer.

ROASTING POTATOES

Roast potatoes are amazingly different when different people cook them. Most people seem to prefer their roast potatoes crisp and brown, not too hard on the outside, and soft and fluffy in the middle.

There are several secrets to beautiful roast potatoes. The first is to blanch (but not cook) them well before you roast them. Peel and cut them to size and put them in a pan of cold water, to which you can add salt if you wish. Bring them to the boil and then immediately turn them off. Drain them and sit them on some paper towel. It is important that they are quite dry when they go into the oven or they will absorb too much fat during cooking and come out soggy. You can scratch the surface of the potatoes with a fork to prevent the skin toughening while they are baking. You should leave them to cool for a few minutes after taking them out of the oven.

You can cook potatoes in the roasting pan along with the meat, if it is being cooked at a fairly high temperature. If the meat is being cooked on a slow heat, tip a little of the roasting fat into another roasting pan about an hour before it is ready, and set the pan on the top shelf of the oven to heat up. About a quarter of an hour later, put the potatoes into the hot fat in this second tin, turning them so that you baste the whole surface. Cook them until they are soft, basting them along with the meat and turning them over after half the time. Do not cover them once they leave the oven — this will make the skins soften.

PUMPKIN IN THE MICROWAVE

It is sometimes hard to understand why pumpkin, so soft and tender when cooked, should be so hard and difficult to deal with when raw.

Using a microwave can take much of the hard work out of cooking pumpkin. Without peeling it, cut it into large, chunky slices and scoop out the seeds. Microwave these slices uncovered, with their fattest sections toward the outside of the dish, for about the time you would take to cook the same amount of potato. When the pumpkin is cooked it is easy to cut into smaller slices and to peel if you wish to. If the skins are soft, however, they can be eaten — vitamins are concentrated under the skin.

RICE

WHITER BOILED RICE

To keep white rice really white during cooking, add a tablespoon of lemon juice to the cooking water. This not only keeps the colour but improves the flavour. For a change of flavour and a colour contrast, toss in some fresh or frozen garden peas when the rice is nearly cooked.

SALADS

Most fresh salads keep well in covered containers in the fridge, provided they do not already have dressing on them. Tomatoes and avocados tend to soften and discolour and can spoil the salad so they should be added fresh and eaten at one sitting. Made-up salads, like potato, rice or vegetable salad in mayonnaise, will usually keep in covered containers if they are not mixed together.

SALADS WITH A DIFFERENCE

Salads are wonderfully healthy and fresh foods, but they can easily become boringly predictable. For a variation on the usual salads, cut up apples, celery, firm peaches, nectarines, pawpaws or melons and mix them with grapes, grapefruit segments, cheese cubes and/or chopped raw nuts. Toss these in a light mayonnaise and garnish with chopped fresh parsley or coriander.

SALADS WITHOUT DISCOLOURATION

Some ingredients in salads and fruit salads are difficult to keep for any length of time once they are cut, because of discolouration caused by the cut surface oxidising. This can be minimised in several ways:
• use stainless steel knives for cutting; or
• put cut vegetables in water until you are ready to make up the salad; or
• squeeze a little fresh lemon juice on cut fruit and cover it with plastic until you are ready to use it.

SAVE TIME PREPARING ROOT VEGETABLES

Chopped and peeled root vegetables keep well in the fridge in plastic bags or fridge canisters. When you know you'll be busy the following day, try preparing enough for two meals and storing half.

For use in salads, vegetables such as carrots keep well just covered with water in a bowl in the fridge. This prevents them drying on the surface. You can chill washed lettuce for a little while in a bowl of iced water in the fridge. Once it is crisp, drain it and it will keep well in the fridge for several days. If you have a special lettuce container, you can store lettuce for 2–3 weeks if necessary. Cut out the stalk and store the lettuce, unwashed, in the container. Wash the leaves you require immediately before use. Always wash and dry the container thoroughly before refilling.

SKINNING TOMATOES

Many recipes call for tomatoes to be skinned before being added. The skins do not cook into dishes and tend to remain as hard, curled up pieces which can spoil a dish. Tomatoes are easy to skin using one of these methods:

• Dip them into boiling water for a few moments. Lift them out with a slotted spoon or dip them wrapped in the kind of greengrocers' plastic net bag you get with your onions or oranges. The skins will come off easily when they are cool enough to handle.

• One by one, skewer them on a carving fork and hold them over a hot plate or burner on the stove for a few moments (the technique is something like toasting marshmallows!). Turn them so that they heat evenly all over. Remove them when they are just heated but not mushy. The hot skins should then come off easily.

• Put them in the freezer for a few days (you can store them this way for months). When they thaw, the skins will peel off with no trouble.

TASTIER PEAS

Peas cooked in the microwave with only a spoonful of water are more nutritious (and keep their colour and texture better) than those boiled in water. If you don't have a microwave, try steaming them over, rather than boiling them in, water. Adding a sprig of mint will improve the flavour, whatever the cooking method. If the peas are not young, a pinch or two of sugar can also be an improvement.

FRUIT

CITRUS FRUIT

REMOVING THE PIPS

Segments of mandarin, orange or grapefruit are a beautiful adornment to many dishes, but having to remove the pips without spoiling the segments can be an off-putting task. To do this, you will need a sharp, pointed knife and a cutting board:

• Hold the segment flat on the board with one hand, with its inside edge (where the pips are) facing toward the other hand (where the knife is).
• Make a small cut across the central seam of the segment (about 1 cm or less) and back to the middle seam.
• Keeping the segment flat on the board, you can now carefully press the pips out through the opening, without damaging the rest of the segment.

CITRUS FRUITS HARD TO PEEL?

If you have difficulty penetrating the tough skin of an orange, lemon or lime, try blanching it for a few minutes in a bowl of hot water before peeling it. The skin should then come away easily.

MORE JUICE FROM UNRIPE FRUIT

If you need fresh lemon juice and have only green, unripe lemons, don't despair. Put them in the oven on 180°C for a short time (until they are warm rather than hot) or in the microwave on High for a minute.

This breaks down the cellulose tissue a little so that when you squeeze them, more juice will be released.

NO WASTE USING CITRUS

Recipes often call for one part of a lemon, lime, orange or other citrus fruit. If the recipe requires only the juice and not the zest, or vice versa, you can save the other parts for another time in your freezer or fridge:

• Save the juice which is not needed by putting it into ice-cube trays and freezing it. You can then thaw it in small quantities as required.
• Save the zest (rind) by either freezing it in a small container or mixing it with caster sugar and storing it in an airtight jar in the fridge.
• Save the pips for jam-making. To use them, tie them in a clean piece of cloth and add them to the fruit during cooking. They are rich in pectin, which helps the jam to set. In their bag they can easily be removed when the jam is cooked.

DRIED FRUIT

PLUMPER, RICHER PRUNES

Prunes can be enriched in all sorts of ways when you cook them for eating. Soak and cook them in one of the following flavourings:

• Unsweetened fruit juice (especially apple or blackcurrant) for an enhanced fruity taste.

• Cold tea for enhanced colour and a stronger prune taste.

• Brandy or cherry brandy for a sophisticated taste treat after a special meal. In this case, soak them well for several days in a covered container in the fridge. You can store them like this, tightly sealed, for months, but don't cook them, as this will make the alcohol content evaporate.

PLUMP DRIED FRUITS BEFORE USING

Sometimes cakes and puddings made with dried fruit tend to be a little dry when they are cooked. This can be because the fruit has dried out considerably in storage and it absorbs some of the liquid from the recipe during cooking. Even so, they may not reconstitute enough to become really tender and delicious. This is especially so in fruit breads and rich fruit cakes.

By reconstituting the fruit to a degree before you use it, your cakes and puddings will be moister and tastier. One traditional solution to this problem is the 'boiled fruit cake', where the fruit is boiled before being added to the cake. But you can get the same effect in a number of ways:

• Put the fruit in a microwave-safe dish and add a little water, fruit juice, port or brandy. A small knob of butter can be good too. Microwave it on High for half to one minute (depending on quantity) and then cover it and leave it aside for at least 15 minutes. During this time the fruit will absorb much of the liquid. Use any residual liquid as part of the quantity in the recipe.

• Put the fruit in a steamer and steam over water for about 15 or 20 minutes. Leave it to stand without opening the lid until it is cool enough to use.

• Just cover the fruit with boiling water and then cover it with a lid or an inverted plate. Allow the fruit to steep in the water for half an hour and then strain it, using the strained water in the recipe liquid content.

CHOP GLACÉ AND DRIED FRUITS

Glacé and dried or candied fruits can be difficult to chop as they have a bad habit of sticking to the knife. To minimise this, rinse the knife in cold water before you start and shake off any excess drops. The fruit will cut more easily.

FRUIT ASSORTMENT

STORE PASSIONFRUIT

When passionfruit are in season, you may enjoy quite a glut, especially if you are growing them in the garden, and it can be hard to use them before they go mouldy. To enjoy them all year round, empty the contents into ice-cube trays and freeze them. When frozen, turn them into a freezer canister with a lid and label them with the date. You can have fresh passionfruit in any season simply by thawing out the number you need.

FRUIT SALADS KEEP BETTER

Make your fruit salads keep better by adding a safe preservative. Dissolve a small-dose vitamin C tablet in the syrup or juice used to moisten the fruit. This will slow the breakdown of the fruit and help it keep its colour longer.

You can use this method with other fruit dishes and in preserved fruits too.

HEALTHY ICE TREAT FOR CHILDREN

In summer, children can be treated to iced foods without harming their health. Roll bananas in chopped nuts, hundreds and thousands, coconut, or whatever you have handy, stick an ice-block stick into each banana at the end and freeze them. They come out with the texture of ice cream and are much better for the children's health than conventional ice cream.

PREVENT CUT FRUIT TURNING BROWN

To prevent apples, bananas, pears or peaches turning brown as you prepare them for a cooked dish, try sprinkling them with lemon juice as you cut them.

OVERRIPE OR WASTE FRUIT

Summer is a wonderful time for fruits, especially soft fruits, but they can ripen too quickly at times. If you see your fruit beginning to ripen faster than your family can eat it, cut it into pieces and make a fruit salad. Place it in a wide-mouthed jar or canister and add a good dash of brandy or liqueur (Kirsch, cherry brandy or Maraschino are good, but use whatever you have as long as it is not a creamy liqueur). Put on a lid and shake the mixture gently. The liqueur will blend with the fruit to make a rich and delicious dessert which will keep for a day or two longer (if it lasts that long!) than the fruit would have done alone.

PINEAPPLE SKIN DRINKS FOR SUMMER

All that cut-away skin from a pineapple needn't be wasted. You can use it to make either alcoholic or non-alcoholic drinks:

• Pineapple Fruit Drink: In a big pan, simmer the skins in water, with sugar or honey to taste and a little lemon or lime juice. When they cool, strain out the solids and add a little fresh chopped mint. Chill thoroughly before serving.
• Pineapple Wine: In a clean plastic bucket, put the skins from several pineapples and a kilogram of sugar, together with a little all-purpose wine yeast (available from health food and brewing shops). Cover the bucket with a clean damp tea-towel and leave it in a cool place for about ten days, while it ferments. Stir it well once a day. Then strain the

liquid into sterilised flagons with a little water lock (also available from health food and brewing shops) to prevent air getting in the top. Leave it in a cool dark place until no more bubbles rise to the surface. Siphon the wine into clean bottles, cork them and leave them for about 6 months before drinking. For a little variety, mix some chopped fresh ginger with the skins in the initial ferment.

OVERRIPE BANANAS MAKE A SPECIAL DESSERT

If your bananas have turned dark brown and soft and you think there's nothing for it but to feed them to the staghorn ferns, hold off. They make a delicious ice dessert with very little trouble.

To 4 overripe bananas, add 3 tablespoons unflavoured yoghurt, 1 tablespoon lemon juice and 2 tablespoons Advocaat liqueur. Blend the mixture in a food processor or blender and, if you like, stir in a spoonful or two of chopped nuts or glacé ginger. Put the mixture into freezer trays and freeze it. Without any further beating, it will set into a delicious ice cream style dessert. Keep it covered and eat it within two days or it will spoil.

FOODS FROM FLOUR

BATTERS AND PANCAKES

FLUFFIER PANCAKES

To make lighter, thinner pancakes, always let the batter stand for at least half an hour (even overnight won't hurt) before cooking. This breaks down the starch, giving a thinner, softer pancake.

If you don't have time, you can use self-raising flour or add a teaspoon of baking powder to plain flour to make light, fluffy pancakes with no standing time required.

Alternatively, your pancakes will come out lighter if you add a couple of teaspoons of rice flour to the mixture. The same can be done with batter for batter puddings.

LIGHTER BATTER FOR FISH

If you love fried fish but do not like a heavy coat of batter, try this. Season a little white or wholemeal flour with a shake of herbs and/or spices. Dip the fish in this, coating it well. Then dip the pieces in beaten egg and put them straight into the frying pan.

A very crisp batter for deep-fried fish (or other foods) can also be made by adding a little yeast to the batter. Dissolve a teaspoon of fresh or dried yeast in a little warmed water and add a tablespoon of oil. Stir in the flour and enough water to give the batter a consistency like thick cream. Beat it until it is smooth, then leave it to stand in a warm place, covered with a cloth, for a quarter to half an hour.

For an even lighter batter, fold in a whisked egg white just before coating the fish.

Another way of lightening a batter is to use crushed ice in a normal batter mixture as part of the liquid allowance. Beat the mixture until it is fluffy and then dip and fry the fish quickly before the batter has a chance to warm up. Alternatively, chill the batter in the fridge for half an hour before using it.

BISCUITS

EVENLY-COLOURED BISCUITS

The secret of keeping your biscuits evenly coloured is in the choice of cooking tray and in where you position the tray in the oven. Dark-coloured trays can absorb too much heat and scorch your biscuits on the bottom.

Trays with high sides prevent the even circulation of hot air and can result in uneven browning of the biscuits across the tin.

Trays which fit too tightly into the oven or which are packed too closely together also block circulation of air and result in uneven cooking of the biscuits. Ideally, trays should have at least 2 cm around them on the shelf. Flat trays allow the best circulation. Unless you have a convection oven which cooks evenly all over, try to divide your shelves evenly into the space available. If the biscuits cook noticeably faster on the upper shelf, be prepared to swap over the trays halfway through baking. (Do this quickly or the oven will cool while the door is open.)

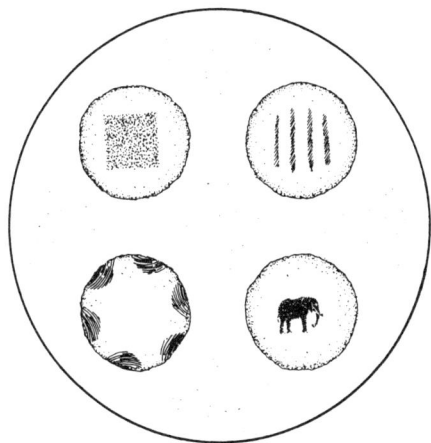

CAKES — SWEET SUCCESS SECRETS

MOISTER CHRISTMAS CAKES

Rich fruit cakes for Christmas, weddings or other special occasions need long, slow cooking and they can often dry out considerably before they are cooked through. Cover the cake with a layer of foil for the last third of the cooking. To do this, cut a sheet of foil before you put the cake in the pan. At the right time, quickly remove the cake from the oven and lightly apply the foil lid, using oven gloves. It need not be completely sealed. The foil will reduce rather than stop the evaporation of steam, and keep the cake moister.

CREAMING BUTTER EASILY

When the butter or margarine sticks fast in a lump to the beater blades and simply whirrs around with them instead of obediently creaming, try heating the beater blades first in hot water and then creaming the butter before the blades have time to cool down. Alternatively, soften the butter or margarine first in the microwave for 5–10 seconds. Baking day might never be the same.

MAKING BETTER BUTTERCAKES

Everyone loves a cake at some time, whether it's a rich, creamy one, a moist fruity one, or any one of hundreds of other kinds. Although there is a bewildering array of packet cakes available today, many people still prefer the taste and texture of a home-made cake, mixed from fresh ingredients. If you avoid doing this simply because you think it is difficult, think again. Cake making is actually easy if you follow some basic rules:
• Arrange the oven shelves as you want them before you preheat the oven.

Leaving this until you go to put the cake in will only cool the oven down again. As a general rule, the lighter and smaller the cake and the higher its recommended cooking temperature, the higher up in the oven it should be, unless you have a convection oven which gives an even heat all over.

• Always heat the oven before you start to make the cake. It must be at its required temperature when the cake is ready to go in or the cake will sink. Light cakes, such as sponges or Swiss rolls, need higher temperatures to set the eggs quickly, while heavier, moister cakes, such as rich fruit cakes or carrot cakes, need a more moderate temperature.

• Take all the ingredients out of the fridge well before you want to make the cake to allow them to warm to room temperature. They will then mix better. Sift the flour with the other dry ingredients before you start to mix the wet ones.

• Beat the butter or margarine and the sugar until they are pale and fluffy. When adding the eggs, reduce the speed of the mixer or food processor. If you can't do this, it may be better to beat in the eggs by hand.

• The eggs should not curdle the mixture if they are at the same temperature as the other ingredients. If there is a sign of curdling, however, immediately add a little of the prepared flour mixture before adding more eggs.

• Stir in the flour, don't beat it in. Beating makes the cake coarse. Always put the mixture lightly and quickly in the tins, without excessive handling or banging. Put it immediately in the pre-heated oven and don't slam the door (or the cake will sink).

• The cake is cooked if it springs back lightly when you touch it or when a skewer pushed into the centre comes out clean. Cool your cake on a wire rack to allow the air to circulate around it.

SWISS ROLLS THAT DON'T CRACK

Do you have trouble with Swiss rolls cracking when you go to roll them up after spreading on the filling? This is caused by the thin cake having dried out too much. To reduce this problem, smooth a damp tea towel over the kitchen bench and sprinkle it with caster sugar. Place the cooked cake onto this to add the filling. Cut off any crisp edges or corners as they will make the cake break when it rolls. (The offcuts are usually popular with the children.) To roll the cake up, grasp the edge of the towel and lift it, easing the

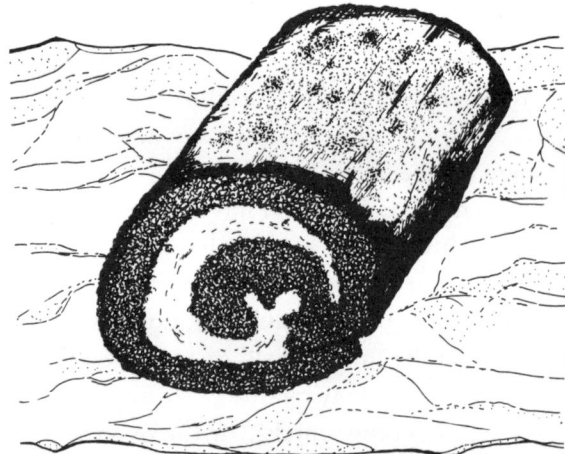

cake over to roll on itself. Continue lifting the edge more and more until it rolls all the way to the other edge.

You can also use this method for rolling up an apple strudel once the filling is spread over the pastry. It is especially good if you are making your strudel with ready-prepared filo pastry, which is very fragile and apt to tear if you try to roll it by hand.

FEATHERLIGHT SPONGES

Have you ever envied someone who can turn out sponges which feel as if they would blow away if the breeze strengthened? There's nothing guaranteed to delight and impress as much as a featherlight sponge, fresh from the oven and decorated with cream and fruit. Here are some tips to help you turn out sponges to marvel at every time:

• Use eggs which have been kept for a few days — they whisk better. Take them out of the fridge well in advance because they increase to greater bulk at room temperature. Whisk them until they are stiff enough to hold a peak. Don't let them get too dry, or they will collapse when they are combined with the other ingredients. The lightness of a sponge comes from the air in the whisked egg so it is critical that this is done well.

• Always heat the oven before you start to make the cake. It should be fairly hot so the cake cooks quickly without drying. Make sure the oven shelves are already in the right place, so you don't lose precious heat re-arranging them when you open the oven to put the cake in. The pans should be greased or lined, ready for use.

• Measure out all the ingredients so the mixture can be quickly prepared once you begin. The whisking of the eggs marks the beginning of the countdown. From this time you need to be as quick as possible or the mixture will start to sink. If everything is ready before this step, you can mix up the cake very quickly and get it straight into the oven.

• For a really light cake, substitute cornflour for about ¾ of the flour in the recipe. If the original recipe specifies self-raising flour, you will need to add some baking powder (about a teaspoon per 125 g of cornflour).

• The flour should be well sifted to separate the grains and incorporate even more air. It is a good idea to have the flour ready in a sifter and sift it over the egg mixture in stages, allowing it to combine evenly. Fold in the flour as quickly and as lightly as you can in a really large bowl to allow plenty of room.

• Use water rather than milk to mix, as this gives a lighter texture and does not break down the air bubbles as much when you mix it in.

• Handle the mixture as gently and as little as possible when putting it into the pans. You may need to shake them gently to even out the top, but avoid knocking or tapping them as this can break down the bubbles. Put the cake into the oven straight away and never slam the oven door shut or the cake will collapse.

CUT SPONGES CLEANLY

When you turn out a really perfect sponge, it is easy to ruin it by cutting it in half for filling. Knives have a nasty way of crumbling the cake or coming through crooked. You can make the layers separately, so you don't have to cut them at all, but this gives you another crust in the middle. Alternatively, use a fine wire cheese cutter, a length of dental floss, or fine fishing trace wire (preferably new!). Twist an end around each index finger, as you would with dental floss, until the wire or cotton is just longer than the width of the cake. Keeping it taut, pull it through the cake in a smooth level movement. Keeping your middle finger tips touching the board while gently guiding your thumbs around the edge of the cake will keep the cut level. The top should then lift off cleanly.

GLACÉ CHERRIES

Glacé cherries have a disappointing tendency to sink to the bottom of a cake during cooking. You can minimise this by putting the cherries in a sieve and rinsing off all the syrup from the surface under cold running water. Cut any large cherries in half before adding them to the mixture. For best results, pat them thoroughly dry on paper towel and then dust them in a little flour before adding them to the mixture. This will help them cling to the flour in the mix and stay where they should be.

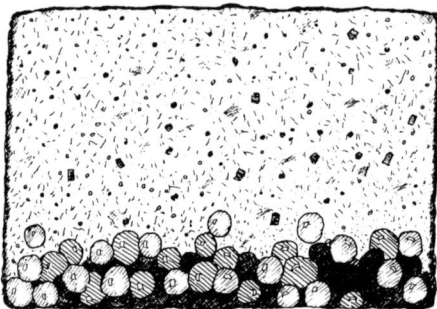

BETTER MICROWAVED CAKES

People are sometimes disappointed with the result the first time they try to cook a cake in the microwave. Don't be put off. It's a very different technique of cooking and you may need to give up some long-held ideas about how to cook cakes.

If your cakes come out raw on the bottom it could be for one of these reasons:

• You may not have cooked it quite long enough. Try giving it a minute longer next time and stick a skewer into the centre. If it comes out clean, the bottom is cooked.

• You may have used a pan which doesn't allow good passage for the microwaves through the bottom. Try elevating the pan (or elevate it more than you did before) during cooking to give the microwaves space to bounce up and cook the underside.

• Cool the cake in its cooking dish for at least 10 minutes before you turn it onto a rack. This prevents drying and allows the cake to finish cooking during its 'standing time'. You can even leave it in the pan until it is only a little warm. It also helps to cover the cake with a plate or cling wrap during cooling.

• If your cakes are too dry, try covering them with an inverted plate for the last few minutes of cooking. Do this quickly to prevent the cake sinking. A glass plate is good, because you can see through it. Dry cakes may be a little overcooked. Try cooking for a minute less next time. You may need to experiment a little to find the right solution. Using a glass cake pan also helps because you can see if the bottom is cooked, so you won't need a further test.

MOUTHWATERING MERINGUES

Depending on the purpose, meringues should either be crisp all through or soft and gooey in the middle with a crisp outside shell. This is entirely a matter of taste, although the use you have in mind will affect your choice. For a fruity pavlova, you may prefer the soft-with-crisp-shell variety, while a pair of meringues with cream in the middle might be better with a more consistently crisp texture.

It's largely a matter of cooking time and temperature. For a pale meringue which is crisp all through, the oven should be about 140–150°C. A hotter oven (about 190°C) and quicker cooking time will give a crisper, browned shell with a softer, marshmallowy centre. At the extreme, the meringue in Bombe Alaska is cooked in a very hot oven in order to keep the ice cream in the centre from melting. This gives a very crisp, browned shell and a very moist under-layer of meringue.

Here are some tips for better results:

• The key to quality meringues is in the way you whisk the egg whites. Make sure the bowl and whisk are really clean. Any trace of fat or oil on either will stop the whites from fluffing up properly.

• Make sure there is no trace of yolk in the white. This contains fat.and will stop the whites whisking well.

• The eggs should not be too fresh. At least 3 days old is best. They should be at room temperature for best results, so if you store your eggs in the fridge, take them out well ahead of time. Whisk them until they are very stiff and dry.

• Always use caster sugar for meringues. Coarser sugar will not dissolve properly in the mixture and will give a gritty texture (and sometimes brown spots) in the meringue. Icing sugar is too fine and will give you royal icing rather than meringue. For a crisp-all-the-way-through meringue, fold the sugar into the whites after they are whisked. For a soft-centred, crisp-shelled meringue, beat the sugar into the whisked egg white gradually.

• Some chefs suggest adding a little cornflour and vinegar or lemon juice to the mixture.

• Make sure the oven is pre-heated to the required temperature before you whisk the eggs. The meringues must go straight into the oven as soon as they are made or they will start to sink.

• Dessert meringue shells filled with cream can be very difficult to cut into portions without cracking. This problem can be solved by filling the shell up to 3 hours before you serve it. This gives the meringue a chance to absorb a little of the moisture from the cream without becoming noticeably soft. (Don't leave it any longer than this or it may become soggy.) The meringue can then be cut without falling to pieces.

PASTRY PROBLEMS

KEEPING THE UNDERCRUST CRISP

It can be quite a problem to keep the bottom crust of a pie from becoming soggy during cooking, especially if you are using a pottery or glass baking dish. These do not transmit the heat as well as metal ones.

If you are making a sweet or savoury open tart or quiche, this problem is easily overcome by baking the crust blind (empty) before adding the filling. Keep the sides from falling in by filling the shell with dried beans or by making a little collar of aluminium foil around the inside of the walls to prop them up during cooking. Remove the beans or the foil for the last five minutes of blind baking to allow the air to get to the pastry.

If you are making a two-crust pie, you can help the underside to cook faster by not overmoistening the filling. When you pre-heat the oven, put a metal baking sheet on the shelf you will be using and put your pie onto this when it goes into the oven. The hot baking sheet will heat the bottom of the dish faster and help to make the undercrust crisper.

FLAKY PASTRY

Good pastry must be made in cool conditions. All the utensils, ingredients and your hands should be as cool as possible. Avoid making it, or use commercial frozen pastry, if the weather is hot. If you have no other choice, try putting the pastry in the fridge (in a plastic bag) for half an hour from time to time during preparation. This gives it a chance to cool down and rest.

Once the temperature is right, there are a few basic rules which will help you turn out good pastry:

• Use firm butter or margarine (rather than one designed for easy spreading) and unbleached bread flour if you can get it.

• Add a teaspoon or two of lemon juice to the water and use only as much water as you need to make a firm dough. Too much will make the pastry tough and flat. The water should be very cold.

• Knead the dough. Flaky pastry, like yeast dough, needs to have the gluten in the flour broken down by good kneading. This helps it keep its texture through the many rollings necessary.

• Take the butter from the fridge a little before starting. It needs to be firm but not rock hard. If you forget, 5 seconds in the microwave can help.

• Rolling is important as it spreads the fat between the layers and traps air inside. Always roll evenly away from you, without turning the pastry over, and never roll right to the edge of the pastry as this allows trapped air to escape from the centre. Roll in short pushes, lifting the pin and putting it down again.

• Don't roll the pastry too thinly at first as this can push the butter through the surface of the pastry, hardening the crust and spoiling the layers. Keep the dough even in size, shape and thickness, rolling it a little thinner each time it is folded over

in thirds. If the butter does start to break through, dust the pastry with flour and rest it in the fridge for 10 minutes before proceeding.

• Always scrape off scraps of pastry from the board between rollings. If they harden and are then rolled into the pastry they will make it lumpy.

• Each time it is folded, seal the edges well by pressing them with your hand or with the rolling pin. Let the pastry rest in the fridge (in a plastic bag) for 10 minutes or so before rolling it again.

• Flaky pastry should be firm and cool before cooking and should be put into a preheated hot oven (about 220°C).

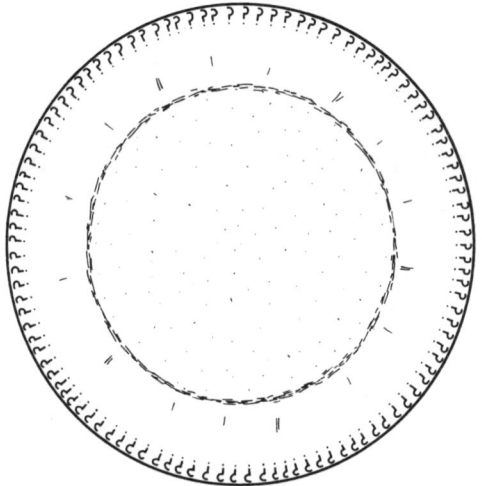

SHORTCRUST PASTRY GRANDMA WOULD HAVE LOVED

Does your spouse ever make passing references to the apple pies mother or grandmother used to make? Do you find yourself envying those hands of yesterday which made the most mouthwatering pastry? There are several secrets to making featherlight shortcrust pastry:

• Use 1 part fat to 2 parts flour. A

proportion of lard in the fat gives a shorter finish. You can use some butter for its flavour if you mix it with a proportion of lard or vegetable shortening. Avoid using all butter because it hardens the pastry.

• A rich short pastry should have about 2 eggs per 500 g of flour. The pastry becomes shorter if you increase the proportion of fat a little.

• Plain flour is usually preferable to self-raising unless you are making a very rich, fatty pastry. A proportion of cornflour instead of some of the flour makes the pastry shorter. You can substitute cornflour for up to a quarter of the flour.

• If you are adding sugar to your pastry and want an even-coloured finish, use the finest sugar you can. Caster or even icing sugar is good. Sugar with larger crystals will often make dark spots on the pastry when it cooks.

• Make sure the liquid added to the flour and fat mixture is as cold as possible. Add only enough liquid to make the dough bind together. Too much liquid will make the pastry hard. A teaspoon or two of lemon juice in the water improves the pastry.

• For two-crust fruit pies with melt-in-the-mouth pastry, use a higher proportion of fat and self-raising flour to lighten the pastry. Use just enough water to make the crumbs into a dough. Try about 250 g of self-raising flour to 150 g of lard (or mixed lard and margarine) to about 2 table-spoons of water. The pastry may be difficult to roll out so rest it in the fridge in a plastic bag before use.

• Handle the pastry as lightly as possible and with cool hands. Pastry goes heavy if it is handled too much. Using a food processor or mixer to rub the fat into the flour gives better results. Otherwise, use a light movement, lifting the mixture to aerate it as you crumble in the fat. Shake the bowl from time to time to bring the larger lumps to the top. Stop rubbing as soon as the fat is incorporated or the pastry will become oily.

• Keep the mixture as cool as possible. If convenient, pastry benefits from a period of resting in the fridge in a plastic bag before it is rolled out. This helps to prevent shrinkage in the oven.

• When putting it in the cooking dish, be careful to drape the pastry generously into shape rather than stretching it across to fit. If you stretch it, it will tend to go back to its original size during cooking.

• Always have the oven preheated to the correct temperature before putting the pastry in. This will set it quickly without distorting.

PASTRY SHORT-CUTS

Many people with busy lives avoid making pastry because it takes too long and makes too much mess. You can reduce this problem by doing much of the preparation in advance, when you have some time to spare, and by making more than you need. You can do this in two ways:

• Make a 'pastry mix', consisting of the fat and flour (usually 1 part fat to 2 parts flour, by weight). You can store this in the fridge or even in the freezer for some time. The added advantage is that the ingredients will always be cool when you want them. When you want to make pastry, just stir in sugar or seasoning if you wish, moisten the mixture with suitable liquid and roll it out.

• Make the pastry up and roll it into a small, thick square. Cover it well with plastic and label it with the date. It will keep in the fridge for a week or two and in the freezer for a few months. Allow it to soften to coolish room temperature before rolling it out and using it.

CAKE FAILURES
SALVAGED

CRUMBLY MERINGUES

Meringues store very well in dry conditions but they easily absorb moisture from the atmosphere, especially if they are not tightly sealed in a container. This can result in your batch of meringues disintegrating into a crumbly mass instead of staying crisp and whole.

If you find your meringues have fallen apart, try crumbling them up further and folding the pieces into whipped cream with fresh strawberries, grapes, mandarin segments or other suitable juicy fruit. This makes a delicious dessert and no-one will know it wasn't planned that way.

OVERCOOKED MICROWAVED CAKES

Microwave cooking is a wonderful time-saver but is a delicate process as far as correct timing of dishes is concerned. If you have ever had a home-made microwave cake come out hard and overcooked, there may be hope for you yet. This treatment is particularly good for cakes which normally have a longer shelf-life, such as fruit, carrot or zucchini cakes:

• Pierce the cake deeply all over with a fine skewer, at about 3 cm intervals.

• Over the surface dribble several tablespoons of port, sweet sherry, brandy, apple juice (preferably concentrated) or a mixture of these. Make sure that the top of the cake is evenly wetted but not too soggy.

• Wrap the cake well in a freezer bag and leave it in the pantry for a day or two. If it is still firm or dry, repeat the treatment. After a few days you should have a beautifully rich and moist cake, often better than the original recipe could have produced!

CAKES THAT SINK IN THE MIDDLE

If your cake sinks in the middle, it can still be turned into a triumph. Sprinkle an eggcupful of sherry, brandy, or port (or a tablespoon of liqueur) over it and set it aside under a sheet of cling wrap while you make a filling.

Prepare some fresh soft fruit — peaches, strawberries, bananas, or whatever you prefer — either one variety or a mixture of complementary ones. Chop them if they are large, remove any seeds and sprinkle them with the same

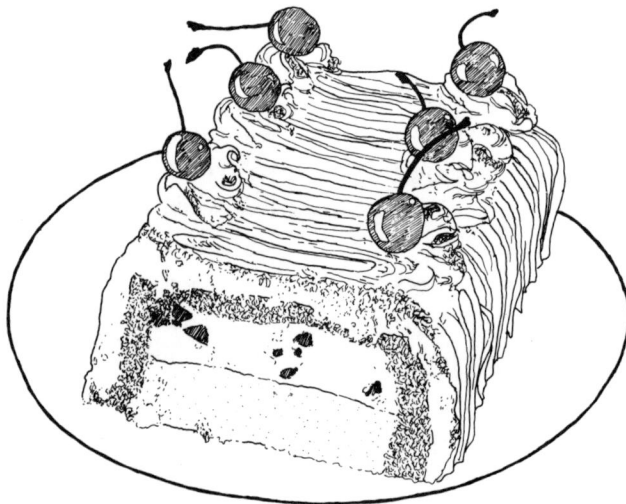

alcohol as the cake. If soft fruit are not in season, you can used drained canned or frozen fruit.

Whip some cream with a little sugar (and, if you like, some finely chopped glacé ginger), until it is fluffy. Pipe this into a bed across the sunken surface of the cake. Top with the fruit and, if you like, decorate it with crumbled chocolate Flake or grated dark chocolate. Serve immediately.

You may prefer to use orange juice to sprinkle on the cake. Another alternative is to sprinkle it with strong chocolate milk and use chopped-up marshmallows and grated chocolate instead of the fruit. Top with chocolate or caramel sauce.

STALE FRUIT CAKE

If your fruit cake becomes stale, you can freshen it in two ways:
• Prick it deeply all over with a fine skewer and then sprinkle it generously with brandy, port, sherry or apple juice. Wrap it well in a plastic bag and put it away for a few days. The liquid will even itself out through the cake and moisten it deliciously again.
• Put a thick slice of fresh bread in the cake tin and close the lid. If the lid is not tight-fitting, put several thicknesses of cling wrap under the lid, sticking out all round. This will seal the opening. Leave the tin for up to 2 days and the cake will absorb the moisture from the bread.

COLLAPSED SOUFFLÉS

A soufflé can often be saved if it collapses as you take it out of the oven simply by returning it there immediately. Usually, it will puff up again in a few minutes and you can try removing it again. Never turn off the oven until the soufflé is safely served. Avoid sudden drafts as you open the door or lift it out — these will certainly make it sink.

Unless you are an expert soufflé maker, it is never wise to advertise to the waiting eaters that the dish they are about to receive is a soufflé. If you don't manage to retrieve a collapse, you will probably spend the rest of the meal apologising or making excuses. It will usually taste delicious anyway and just have a firmer texture than you planned, but you will probably feel terrible.

The secret is to be evasive about the meal. If the soufflé succeeds, it will arouse applause. If it collapses before you get it to the table, quickly sprinkle a generous amount of grated cheese, chopped nuts, chives or other topping on the surface and brown the top under the grill or in the oven. Call the dish a fluffy omelette, a South American pudding or a Mongolian custard, according to the texture you have achieved. Everyone will find it delicious and you will be the only one who expected something else.

STALE BREAD CAN BE REVIVED

Unsliced bread can be refreshed when it goes a little stale by briefly cooking it again. Sprinkle it with water, wrap it in foil and heat it in the oven on 200°C for about 5–10 minutes (depending on the size of the loaf). Allow it to cool before unwrapping it, unless you are taking it straight to the table.

TASTY TREATS FROM STALE BREAD

Beat an egg (or several if you are feeding a few people) with about a tablespoon of milk per egg and use it to make these treats from stale bread or sandwiches:
• Slices of bread (either fresh or stale) can be turned into a delicious treat for breakfast or brunch, especially with eggs, bacon, tomatoes, mushrooms and/or sausages. Soak both sides of the bread thoroughly in the egg mixture, then fry the bread in oil, margarine or butter until

golden brown. Drain it briefly on a paper towel before serving.

• Alternatively, use a glass to cut the bread into rounds to fit patty cases, soak it in the egg mixture and lightly press into the greased patty-case tins. Cook them in a hot oven for about 10 minutes. When cooked, the cases can be used for sweet or savoury fillings.

• You can even turn leftover sandwiches into a tempting treat in the same way. Dip the sandwiches into beaten egg mix or drizzle the egg over them with a teaspoon, coating both sides. Then fry them until they are golden brown. If it is too difficult to coat the sandwiches, just spread the outsides well with butter or margarine and fry them in a good non-stick pan with no oil. This way the outside will toast and the fillings will soften and seem fresher again.

STORING FOOD

FLOUR

To prevent weevils from developing in your flour, put it into the freezer for a few days as soon as you buy it. Unless you mean to use the whole lot immediately, it is not advisable to add fresh flour to old in a storage container, especially if it is wholemeal, which contains natural oils and can turn rancid. It is best to wash the container and dry it thoroughly before refilling it with fresh flour.

YEAST COOKERY

BAKING BREAD:
TESTING IF IT'S DONE

Everyone loves the smell of bread straight from the oven. Cooking it just the right amount may sometimes seem difficult. Too little and it may be doughy in the middle.

Too much and it can be dry and go stale quickly. To check whether it is quite done, lift it out of its pan and tap the bottom lightly with your knuckles. If it is done, it should sound hollow. If you feel that the crust underneath is not as crisp as you would like when you do this, put it back in the oven without its pan for the last 5–10 minutes. The bottom will crisp up nicely.

HOME-MADE DAMPER

Damper is bread made with bicarbonate of soda instead of yeast. It was made in the days when it was impossible to get yeast in the bush. To make damper rise better, use buttermilk, sour milk or yoghurt (thinned down if necessary with fresh milk) to mix the dough, instead of water. This increases the production of the carbon dioxide bubbles which make the dough rise.

TASTIER WHOLEMEAL BREADS

For a subtly different taste to your wholemeal bread, try substituting whey (strained from fresh yoghurt or home-made soft cheese), tea, beer or fruit juice for some of the liquid in your recipe.

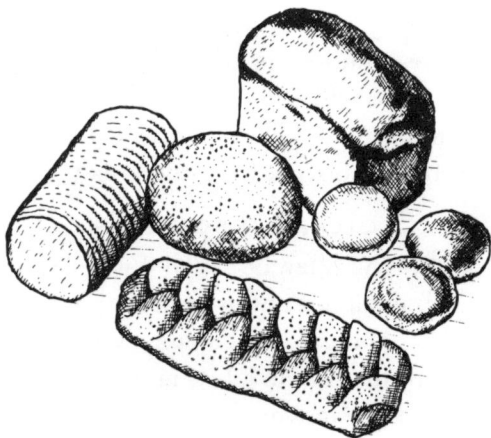

SURFACE FINISHES FOR BREAD

One of the nicest things about home-made bread, apart from the cooking smell, is the way it looks when it comes from the oven. You can improve the appearance of your bread in all sorts of ways by accentuating the crustiness, giving it a shiny surface or texturing it with seeds or grains.

Some glazes used on big loaves which need long cooking can burn to an overly dark colour before the bread is done, spoiling the result. These are best brushed on towards the end of the cooking. Don't keep the loaf out of the oven too long, however, as this can spoil the bread.

SOFTENING GRAINS FOR WHOLEMEAL BREAD

If you have ever tried making bread with whole grain without softening the grain first, you may have chips on your teeth to prove it. Whole grains sold in the shops are usually pretty well dried out. They will rob some of the moisture from the dough and may make it too dry, but there is not likely to be enough moisture to reconstitute them properly.

To make your whole-grain bread moist and tender, pre-cook the grains the day before you want them. To ½ cup (90 g) of whole grain, add ¾ cup (180 ml) of water

TOPPING	EFFECT
Water sprayed from a mist sprayer	Increases crispness of crust
Salt water sprayed on	Hard, pale, crisp crust
Cream or milk brushed on	Gives a golden crust
Beaten egg brushed on near end of cooking	Shiny, dark brown surface
Egg yolk brushed on	Dark glaze to white breads
Egg white brushed on	Crisp, shiny crust
Melted butter or oil brushed on	Soft, pliant crust
Syrup or honey brushed on late in cooking	Sticky glaze to sweet/fruit breads
Poppy, sesame, celery, caraway seed	Add taste and decoration
Cracked whole grains sprinkled on	Add texture and decoration

(or increase the quantities proportionately for a big batch of bread).

If you make bread often, you can cook a big batch of grains and freeze them, taking out enough early in the morning each baking day.

• To cook grains on the stove top: Cover the pan and bring it to the boil. Turn it down to the lowest setting and let it just simmer for half an hour. Turn it off and let it cool without opening the lid.

• To cook grains by microwave: Put the ingredients into a large microwave jug or dish with a lid. Microwave it on High for 3 minutes and then on Medium for 20 minutes. (For each additional ½ cup of grain, increase the time on High by 1 minute and on Medium by 5 minutes.) Leave the grains to stand without opening until they have cooled.

The grain can be mixed with the flour for the bread dough at any time after it has cooled to gentle warmth. If it is stored in the fridge before use, it may benefit from warming slightly first, either in the microwave or by mixing it with the recipe liquid which, in this case, would be slightly hotter than usual. Any leftover liquid from cooking can be added into the recipe water.

SAUCES AND SOUPS

SAUCES — SWEET AND SAVOURY

PREVENTING CURDLING IN CUSTARDS OR EGG SAUCES

Custards and sauces thickened with egg must be heated very slowly over water and stirred constantly, to prevent them curdling. Any acid ingredients (such as lemon juice) may make them curdle no matter how careful you are with the cooking process.

To reduce their tendency to curdle, add a tablespoon of cornflour, mixed to a paste in some of the liquid in the recipe, at the beginning of cooking. This makes the mixture less likely to separate.

If your sauce does curdle, you can often salvage it by rapidly whisking it, off the heat (see *Dairy Foods and Eggs*).

FRENCH-STYLE THICKENING

Traditional French cooking uses a mixture of flour and butter called *beurre manié* to thicken sauces. The rich taste of butter is characteristic of much classical French cooking and gives it an unmistakable flavour.

To make *beurre manié*, knead together equal quantities of plain flour and butter. You can do this in a food processor. Store this in tablespoon-sized pieces in a tightly-sealed jar in the fridge until you need them. Take out one or two pieces a little ahead of time so they can warm to room temperature.

To use the mixture, take the sauce to be thickened off the heat and make sure it is no longer boiling. Stir in one piece of *beurre manié* until it dissolves. The butter will melt into the sauce, taking the flour with it, so that it is most unlikely to form lumps. When the mixture has disappeared into the sauce, return it to the heat and stir until it thickens. If necessary, you can repeat the procedure until the sauce has reached the right consistency.

LUMPY SAUCES

What an embarrassment it is when a sauce which should have been velvety smooth decides instead to become chunky! It is not a lost cause, however. Put the sauce in a blender or food processor, or beat it with a hand-held electric beater, egg-whisk or milkshake mixer for a minute and it will become smooth again. (If you are beating it in a non-stick saucepan, be careful not to touch the sides, or you will remove the non-stick coating.) You may need to reheat it gently before serving.

MAKING A ROUX

Classical sauces are often based on a roux. This is a mixture of fat (usually butter) and flour which is cooked separately before the liquid is added.

To make a roux, melt the butter over a low to medium heat and then stir in the flour, stirring the mixture over the heat until it sizzles. If you are making a white sauce, don't let the mixture brown. If you are making a brown sauce, you can sizzle it gently until it has a good colour.

Remove it from the heat and add the liquid, a little at a time, stirring well. The secret is to add the liquid off the heat and in very small amounts, and to stir briskly as you do. This way the sauce will be smooth and creamy instead of lumpy. Continue adding liquid until the sauce reaches the consistency you want, returning it to the heat from time to time (still stirring) between additions of liquid, to reheat it.

QUICK DESSERT SAUCES

For a quick, hot dessert for a winter meal, try mixing an instant pudding with hot milk and serving it immediately with a hot sponge pudding. You can spike it, if you like, by adding liqueur, fruit juice, nutmeg, honey, malt, chopped nuts, coconut or grated chocolate.

Alternatively, purée a can of apricots, plums or cherries with half a cup of crystallised ginger in the blender or food processor and heat it in a saucepan or in a jug in the microwave. Pour this over the sponge for a different delight.

SKINLESS SAUCES

In a busy kitchen it is often convenient to make up sauces, custards and gravies ahead of time, rather than frantically trying to prepare them when everything else is waiting. The penalty can be a sauce with an unappetising skin on the top. To prevent the skin from forming, put a piece of cling wrap over the top and pat it down so that it touches the whole surface.

Make sure the pan is off the heat. (If you want to keep the pan on the heat, use grease-proof paper instead.) The film will help the sauce to stay hot while you prepare the rest of the meal and will stop a skin from forming. Lift it off just before serving.

THICKENING THE TASTY WAY

Soups and stews are warming and delicious on a cold night. While there are many products on the market now for thickening and adding flavour, these often contain considerable salt and artificial flavours, which are not always welcomed in a healthy diet these days. But thickening with flour can give food a floury taste which is not appetising either. Here are some alternatives for making dishes hearty and thick:

• Use pea or lentil flour, available from health food shops, for thickening. Make this up into a paste with some water and gradually thin it, then add it to the mixture, stirring well. Simmer it for a little while until it thickens up. It adds a good flavour as well as protein to the dish.

• Use tomato paste to thicken a little as well as add flavour, stirring in well and simmering (without a lid, if necessary) to reduce the fluid further.

• Add plenty of grated or finely chopped vegetables and/or a good handful of lentils, pearl barley, dried peas or soup mix at the beginning of cooking. As the mixture cooks, these will swell and thicken the sauce or soup.

• Stir in smoothly-mashed potato until it is well combined, or add some instant powdered potato and stir it in well.

• A spoonful or two of peanut butter (or other nut butter) stirred in also provides some thickening and lots of flavour.

MEAT SOUPS IN A TRICE

Home-made soups undoubtedly taste better than commercial soups and are usually more nutritious. But they can take such a long time to cook.

If you have a good stock as a base, or perhaps plenty of meat juices from a previous dish, try processing the meat and vegetables for the soup together in a food processor or mincer and then simmering them in the stock. The soup will be ready much faster and will not need any further straining or processing.

TANGY TOMATO SOUP

Tomatoes are usually readily available at low prices during the summer so this is a good time to make big batches of tomato soup. You can eat the soup immediately or freeze it for the winter when such things are a luxury.

To give your tomato soup a really delicious flavour, try adding the grated zest and juice of half an orange (or a dash of commercial, unsweetened concentrated orange juice) and two or three rashers of cooked lean bacon into the soup at the start. Process the soup in a blender or food processor when it is cooked to make it smooth. Just before serving you can stir in a little fresh or sour cream or unflavoured yoghurt.

OVER-SALTED SOUP

Most things in cooking are governed by the rule, 'You can put more in but you can't take it out'! Fortunately, salt isn't always one of these. A raw potato in the soup will usually absorb a proportion of the salt. Peel a large potato and cut it into quarters. Put it in the soup and cook it for about 15–20 minutes. Take out the potato and the salt level will be reduced. The now-cooked potato is often delicious too!

ODDS AND ENDS

KEEPING FOOD FRESH

MILK

Milk keeps better in its original pack. If you transfer it to an open jug for serving, use it quickly and don't return the remainder to the pack or it will quickly sour the rest of the pack.

If you have no refrigerator, you can keep milk or cream a little cooler by immersing the pack in a bowl of cool water in a cool place. If the water temperature is cooler than the air temperature it will slow down the rate of souring.

Homogenised milk (in cardboard cartons) can be frozen and kept that way for months. To thaw, simply take it out of the freezer the night before, or microwave it on High for about 8-10 minutes per litre. You will need to give it a good shake before opening the carton as the cream tends to separate out a little during thawing. It may not keep as long as fresh milk once it has been thawed.

CHEESE

If cheese develops a blue mould, don't worry; this is not harmful. If you don't want to eat it, simply scrape it off before serving. Hard cheeses can be kept for weeks in a cool pantry if they are coated with wax. Simply melt some candle wax on a low heat, then dip the cheese in it, making sure the coating around it is sealed. For best results, mix the wax with a little lard or beeswax to make it more pliable. Avoid using scented or insect repellent wax, as this may contain toxic ingredients. Set the waxed cheese to dry on a sheet of freezer plastic, then store it away. If the wax coating breaks and mould develops inside, scrape away the wax and mould, then wipe the cheese with a strong solution of salt in water and recoat it in wax.

EGGS

Fresh eggs can be stored in the refrigerator for at least two weeks, often longer. They should be stored with the pointed end down in the body of the refrigerator, where they will be less exposed to flushes of warm air from the opening of the door.

To be sure you are not adding a bad egg to a dish, always break each one into a cup and smell it first before adding it to the other ingredients. Otherwise you may have to throw away all the other ingredients and start again.

FRESH FRUIT AND VEGETABLES

Most soft fruit and green vegetables will keep longer in the refrigerator — up to a week or so. For best results, don't leave them in plastic bags. Wash them if necessary, but make sure they are well drained and fairly dry before putting them in a covered canister or in the crisper in the refrigerator. Salad vegetables are best if covered, but not sealed, so air can circulate around them. Many vegetables keep longer stored in the refrigerator in special plastic vegetable bags. These bags have microscopic pores to allow some moisture to evaporate. This prevents the vegetables sweating, as they do in conventional plastic bags.

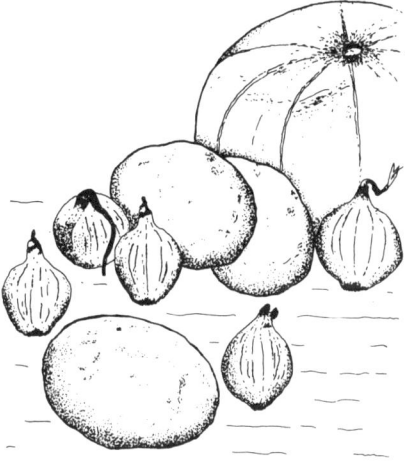

Onions, potatoes, whole pumpkins and other dry-skinned vegetables keep best in an airy basket or rack in a dark pantry. Don't expose potatoes to the light in storage or they will turn green and sprout. This green pigment is poisonous and should be cut off the potato before use.

Mushrooms contain a high proportion of water. As a result, they tend to sweat in a sealed container and will go off rather quickly. To prevent them sweating, store them in the refrigerator in an uncovered container which is lined with a layer or two of paper towel. They may dry out a little after a day or two but will remain fresh for at least a week. As they dry out, they are still perfectly good for cooking although they might be less attractive in a salad.

Keep olives fresh by storing them covered in water in a glass jar. Change the water regularly to keep the olives from discolouring.

Apples, pears, oranges, bananas, pineapples, passionfruit and other dry-skinned fruit are best stored at room temperature, away from the sun. If you want fruit to ripen, standing it in the sun will help. To ripen fruit more quickly, put it in a paper bag in a warm place.

Passionfruit can be kept longer by scooping them out into freezer trays and freezing them. Take them from the trays when they are fully frozen and store them in a sealed canister in the freezer to prevent them drying out. They will thaw quickly when you want to use them, and are as good as fresh passionfruit in cooking.

Bananas can be refrigerated if they begin to overripen but the skins will blacken very quickly. This doesn't spoil the banana, which is still good, especially for cooking or for using in made-up dishes like fruit salads. You can even freeze bananas. Remove their skins and put several in a freezer bag, sealing the top. When thawed they are excellent in dishes such as banana cakes or ice cream.

Pears and Apples: how to keep their colour

When cutting up pears and apples for preserving, you may be racing against time to prepare them all before they go brown. If you have a lot of fruit, it is a battle you can't win simply through speed.

Have a large basin of water beside you and put the prepared fruit pieces into this, ensuring that they are covered by the water. This will keep them from browning until you are ready to use them at the next stage.

MEAT AND FISH

Fresh meat and fish will keep only a day or two, even in the refrigerator. Meat will keep longer if you rinse away any blood on the surface and then wipe it dry with a piece of paper towel.

If the surface of meat becomes slippery and slightly smelly after a short stay in the refrigerator, this indicates that bacteria are already becoming active on the surface. If it has not progressed into the body of the meat, you can freshen it up before cooking by rinsing it well in cold water and patting it dry with some paper towel. Then cook it by searing the outside in a hot pan at the start, to kill any bacteria on the surface. Don't use meat or fish which has become noticeably smelly.

Cooked meat or fish will keep for several days in the refrigerator if it is well sealed from the air. However, you should discard it immediately if it begins to smell unpleasant. When reheating, make sure it is heated through as quickly as possible. Bacteria can grow quickly in the food if it is reheated slowly or incompletely.

Meat and fish will, of course, keep well in the freezer. Always clean and gut fish before freezing as the bacteria in the gut will multiply rapidly as the fish thaws and will spoil the flesh.

Cured meat or fish (salted or smoked) can be kept for up to a week or even more in the refrigerator. If you want to store such food always check the use-by date before you buy.

FLOURS, BAKING INGREDIENTS AND CEREALS

In general, foods such as cereal products, dried fruits, baking powders, dried milks and dried beans should be stored in a cool pantry in airtight jars or containers. They will keep much better if they are dry and leaving them in paper packets will allow moisture to be absorbed. These products can last up to a year if well stored.

However, wholegrain cereals and flours should not be stored for long as they contain oil which can go rancid after a while. These products store well in the refrigerator or the freezer as long as they are in well-sealed containers.

Weevils and Moths
Weevils in the flour are a traditional scourge of the kitchen and are also a hazard in any grain or pulse food stored in a dry state. So too are those little moths which emerge from the packages to fly around the pantry when you are not there.

None of these insects are actually dangerous, and you could eat them if you wanted to without ill effect, but most people find the appearance and the idea of them rather unpalatable.

They usually come with the package in the form of tiny eggs which you can't see. Once they are in the pantry they can eat their way in and out of plastic packages with ease. They can even infest packets of pasta, papadums or other prepared dry foods you may be storing.

There are several ways to prevent their contaminating your food:
• When you bring home packages of flour, dry grains or pulses, put them in the freezer for 48 hours before transferring them to the pantry. You can put the flour packages in a plastic bag, if you like, to keep them dry.
• Alternatively, put them in the microwave for 1–2 minutes on High. (If the package is large, you may need to open it and spread the contents out on a dish to ensure that the microwaves get into all the contents.) If you don't have a microwave, the oven

will do, on Moderate heat for 10 minutes or so. Beware of dry foods which contain oil, like nut products, or those which can be cooked in the microwave, like popcorn and some types of papadums. You may find that they are cooking while you are trying to preserve them!

• After either method of processing, put the food (once it has returned to room temperature) into airtight storage jars to prevent re-infestation from any bugs which are already resident in your pantry. Glass with a good lid keeps the food best, but you may prefer plastic if you have a hard floor and small children.

• A bay leaf inside an airtight jar of dry food can also prevent weevils developing.

• If you are too late and the bugs are already there, sieve the food to remove any developed insects and spoiled food.

Larger grains and pulses can be cleaned without sieving. Shake them in a bowl of water and the insects or cocoons will rise to the surface. Pick (or scoop) them off and repeat the treatment until no more rise to the surface. If you are not going to use the food straight away, dry it thoroughly by spreading it on a baking tray and heating it in a warm oven before you store it again .

Put the good portion of the food in the freezer or in the microwave to kill any remaining eggs. The food is still perfectly safe to use, provided it is not obviously spoiled.

• It is a good idea to have your pantry treated with a safe pesticide if there is a bad infestation. To do this without danger, it is best to call in a professional. At the very least, make sure that any insecticide you use is clearly labelled as safe to use near food. Many pesticides can contaminate your food with chemicals which will harm you, but which do not have an obvious effect immediately. As a precaution, make sure all food is removed from the pantry before you spray. Even safe packaging such as cans can be a hazard. Although the pesticide will not penetrate, traces of it on the can may transfer to your hands and then to the food.

FREEZING AND THAWING

LABELLING FROZEN FOOD

Have you ever gone to your freezer and pulled out an irregularly shaped bag containing an unidentifiable brown something? Or do you have a number of similar-looking, sealed containers in your freezer filled with a variety of foods such as lemon juice, passionfruit, tomato paste and sauces which you have frozen in ice-cube trays?

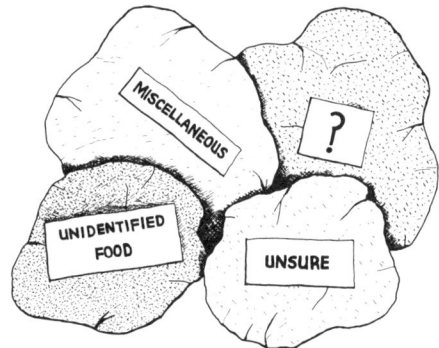

It is always a good idea always to label foods you store in your freezer with the contents, the amount and the date. You will then know exactly what is there and if it has been in the freezer too long for its own good.

If you have a big freezer it is useful to keep an inventory of what you put in. Just add each new item to the bottom of the list. When you take out something, cross it off the list. You are then much less likely to find packages in there which are several years old.

FROZEN FOODS SHAPED FOR REHEATING

Have you ever struggled to find a dish which will hold the contents of an irregularly-shaped plastic bag of frozen food?

Try freezing the bag and its contents in a round freezer canister. You can also use a freezer-safe cooking dish as a mould, as long as the sides go straight up or widen towards the top. If it narrows somewhere above the base, the bag of food will not come out when it is frozen and the dish will be out of circulation until you thaw the food out!

When the food is frozen, lift the bag out of the canister and store it in the freezer as normal. (If the canister is reluctant to come off, stand it in a sink of luke-warm water for a few minutes until the food slips out. Don't leave it too long or the food will thaw on the outside and may spoil.)

This method is particularly good for freezing soup, which is difficult to freeze in a bag without it leaking. The bags are convenient to stack and do not tie up too many canisters in the freezer. For reheating, simply sit them in a dish that is the same shape but a little larger than the one in which they were frozen.

THAWING FOODS IN THE MICROWAVE

The shape of frozen food is also important in microwave defrosting. Flat, round dishes thaw more evenly and quickly than oddly-shaped or thick dishes.

Any package of food which is thick should be turned frequently during thawing to present new sides of the food to the microwaves. Otherwise some parts may cook before others have thawed.

Foods which can be broken up during thawing (such as minced beef, prawns and chopped vegetables) should be separated as soon as possible, to prevent them cooking on the outside before the middle is thawed. Keep them covered to prevent them drying out.

REHEATING CASSEROLES AND STEWS

Cold casseroles and stews are a potential breeding ground for bacteria if they are not treated carefully. Reheating them slowly can encourage the growth of germs which can spoil the food and cause sickness. To be sure they are safe, bring them quickly to boiling point, then simmer them, just off the boil, for about 15 minutes. This will kill any undesirables in the food. Alternatively, heat the food in a microwave quickly to boiling point and then cook it on a Medium or lower setting for at least 10 minutes.

LEMON ICE CUBES

If you have a glut of lemons and want to preserve the juice, freeze it in ice-cube trays. When frozen, transfer the cubes to a sealed freezer canister and label it. When you need lemon juice, you can simply take out as many cubes as you need.

ROCK HARD ICE CREAM

If your freezer is so efficient that it turns your ice cream into rock, soften it before serving by microwaving it on High for up to 2 minutes, in 30-second bursts, testing it in between. Alternatively, take it out of the freezer 30 minutes ahead of time and soften it in the refrigerator. Thawing it on the kitchen bench in warm weather tends to make the outside melt before the middle has softened.

FREEZE TOMATO PASTE

Opened tomato paste sometimes seems to grow mould almost as you look at it. If you like the economy of buying large jars or cans of tomato paste but don't use it fast enough to stop it going mouldy, here's a solution. When you first open the jar, use what you want, then freeze the remainder in ice-cube trays. When the cubes are frozen, transfer them to a labelled, sealed freezer canister or plastic bag to stop them dehydrating and, hey presto! — you have small quantities of paste whenever you need them. The frozen paste can be added to most dishes without thawing, but if you need it thawed it takes only a little while at room temperature and even less in the microwave.

SWEET THINGS

CUMQUAT LIQUEUR

Do you have a cumquat tree which looks very pretty and provides you regularly with lots of inedible little fruit that you don't know how to use? For a very special liqueur which is easy to make, you will need a very large glass (or stoneware) jar with a well-fitting top, some sugar and a bottle (or two, if you have a lot of cumquats) of cheap brandy.

- Choose a jar which is big enough to hold all the ingredients you propose to use, or divide them between several jars.
- You will need about 500 g–1 kg cumquats to a bottle of brandy and about the same weight of sugar as cumquats.
- Prick the cumquats all over with a metal skewer — perhaps 8–12 punctures per fruit. This will allow the brandy and juice to mix.
- Put the pierced cumquats into the jar(s) and add the sugar. Pour over enough brandy to cover the fruit, then fasten the lid. Store the jar(s) in a cool pantry for about 6 months without opening them. You can give them a swish around every month or two if you wish.
- When the time comes to open the bottle, strain off the liqueur into sterilised bottles or decanters. You can drink it immediately but it improves if left for another few months.
- Use the brandied cumquats (complete with their skins) in steamed puddings or marmalade, or roll them in sugar and bake them at 180°C for an exotic dessert. They are particularly good served with yoghurt or ice cream.

BROWN SUGAR WITHOUT LUMPS

Do you avoid brown sugar, despite its taste, because you can't bear to hammer away at the lumps? If you want to use brown sugar but you know it is lumpy, measure out what you need the day before and cover it with a damp cloth overnight. This will soften the lumps.

Alternatively, put the sugar in a glass or plastic jug with a piece of apple and cover it with cling wrap. Cook it in the microwave for 15–30 seconds on High. Repeat, if necessary, until the lumps begin to soften, making sure you check it each time to stop it melting completely.

You can prevent the lumps forming by

storing the sugar in a sealed container in the refrigerator. This will keep it moist.

CARAMEL WITHOUT STIRRING

Do you love caramel tarts and toppings but hate stirring them for ages while they cook? Do you find that pre-prepared caramel toppings don't quite have the creamy taste you want? Try putting a can of sweetened condensed milk in a pressure cooker and adding water up to the top of the can. Pressure cook it for 30 minutes, then let it cool enough to open the can safely. (If it is too hot it may explode when you open it.) The can will contain a delicious caramel topping. You can use it still warm or transfer it to a refrigerator container for use over several days.

HONEY PROBLEMS

Too thick to spoon out

Rich, natural honey brings a taste and smell of the countryside into the kitchen. The better it is, however, the more difficult it can be to spoon accurate quantities out of the jar, especially when you need to measure it carefully for a cake or sweetmeat.

If you have a microwave, the easiest way to solve the problem is to put the whole jar in (provided it is made of glass or plastic and does not have gold ink on the label), without the lid, and microwave it on High in bursts of about 15 seconds. It will rapidly become thin, before it is really hot, and will then spoon easily out of the jar. If it comes in a tin, put a larger quantity than you think you need into a glass or plastic container before microwaving it. You can then measure it accurately when it thins.

If you don't have a microwave, put a large blob which seems more than you want into a small saucepan and stir it over a low heat until it thins. Measure it out as you need and return the remainder to the jar. It will return to its normal condition as it cools. Don't worry if you overheat it. It may crystallise a little afterwards but this will not harm the honey.

Honey, treacle or syrup: a problem to measure

Thick sugary substances like honey, treacle, molasses or syrup, can be difficult to measure because they tend to leave much of their substance behind on the spoon or the scales pan. There are various ways to prevent this. Here are some suggestions:

• Dip your measuring spoon or cup measure into cooking oil and shake off the excess drops. Now, when you measure out your quantity, it will slide cleanly off the spoon.

• You can dust your measure with flour instead for a similar result, but this is not as reliable as the oil method.

• Alternatively, dip the spoon into hot water immediately before measuring each spoonful. The quantity will slide off the spoon.

Use the same methods to prevent these sticky substances from sticking to your scales pan.

JELLIES

Jelly Sets Faster

If you want to make jelly but have left it later than you should, you may still have time.

If you have a good freezer and your memory is good, or if you have a good loud kitchen timer, you can cover your freshly made, hot jelly with cling wrap and put it into the freezer for a little while, checking it after 15 minutes and then after every 5 minutes or so until it has set. (The frequent checking is to prevent it going too far and freezing, which will spoil the texture.)

However, if you are concerned about spoiling the other food in the freezer, or simply don't have the room, find a bowl big enough to stand your jelly mould in with room to spare. Stand the filled jelly mould in it and fill the space outside the mould with ice cubes or crushed ice, a couple of handfuls of salt and enough water to bring the top of this mixture to

the same level as the jelly in the mould. In earlier times, before refrigerators, this was how ice cream was made. The salt will bring the water temperature down towards the temperature of the ice, and the jelly will set quite quickly. (If you have put a really hot jelly mixture into your mould, you may need to replenish the ice from time to time as it will melt before the jelly sets.)

Quick Jelly Masking

To coat the inside of a mould with jelly so that added decoration will stay neatly in place, sit the mould in a bowl of ice cubes or put it into the freezer while you prepare the jelly mixture. When the jelly is ready to pour, the mould should be quite cold. Pour the jelly in and swirl it around. It should set quickly around the sides. You can then decorate the mould with fruit or whatever you choose before pouring in the main filling.

Suspending Fruit in Jelly

Do your generous pieces of fruit always sink to the bottom of the jelly? Do you avoid cutting them into smaller pieces (to help prevent their sinking) because you like the look and taste of bigger chunks? Try letting the jelly set until it is softly gelled before you stir in the fruit. Make sure the fruit is well drained. Put the dish into the refrigerator immediately so that the jelly doesn't melt after you add the fruit. The fruit will then tend to stay where it is put.

For a really professional touch, make the jelly in layers. It takes time but it's worth it. Prepare your mould by coating the inside with a layer of jelly (see this page). Cut the first layer of fruit and arrange it on the jelly layer in the bottom of the mould. Pour over enough cooled but liquid jelly to cover this layer of fruit and put it into the refrigerator to set. When set, repeat the process with a second layer of fruit and jelly and chill again. Continue adding layers of fruit and jelly, chilling between layers, until you have filled your bowl. You can build up with different types of fruit or even different types of jelly. The result will be a truly sumptuous dessert.

Gelatine Without Lumps

Ever had your powdered gelatine develop lumps which were difficult to melt out when you were stirring in the hot water? You can avoid this by first soaking the gelatine in cold water for a little while. This will allow the grains to swell and soften. Then either put the bowl over a basin of hot water and stir the gelatine until it melts or microwave it in 30-second bursts, stirring well in between, until it melts.

Flummery is Easy

Flummery (a light, fluffy jelly) makes a pleasant change from normal jelly in children's meals. Make up a jelly as normal and allow it to set until it is softly gelled. Separate two eggs and whisk the whites until they are stiff, but not too dry. Fold these into the jelly and chill it immediately. (You will get a very pleasant but less fluffy effect simply by adding the egg whites directly to the partly-set jelly and whisking them briskly together.)

Novelty Double-decker Jelly for Children

Children always like something which looks fun. Here is one of our family ideas which originated when, as a toddler, I threw the yolks into a flummery my mother was making! (Children like inventing their own dishes too!)

Make a regular jelly and let it set until it is just gelled but not yet firm. Quickly whisk in a whole egg with a rotary beater or a hand-held electric whisk. As the jelly sets, it will settle into two layers - a milky layer containing the yolk and a fluffy layer containing the white. This is a sure-fire success at children's parties.

FOOD COLOURING CONTROLLED

There's nothing which brings to mind the old adage that 'you can put more in but you can't take it out' so much as food colouring. Too much food colouring in a dish can turn it from a subtle sensation to a technicolour nightmare. It might please the children, but the rest of the family probably won't touch it. No matter how careful you are, there are always those times when 5 drops instead of 1 launch themselves from the bottle on an irrevocable course into a new rainbow-coloured dish.

To be sure you don't get more than you bargained for, try dipping a skewer into the bottle of colouring and shaking the drops from the end of the skewer into the dish. This way you can never get too much at a time. It may take a little longer to reach the desired hue, but it won't end in a tragic accident.

GLOSSIER CHOCOLATE DECORATIONS

Really beautiful desserts can be prepared with cooking chocolate decoration, but it is very disappointing when the chocolate develops a dull surface with white patches as it cools. Excessive cooking is usually the culprit.

To prevent this, the chocolate should be cut or grated into small pieces before melting so that it will melt evenly. Melt it slowly, so that you have control over the softening, and heat it only until it is just melted. Do this either in a basin over a pan of water simmering on a low heat, or in the microwave on Medium power. Stir it gently, continuously if over heat, or each 20–30 seconds if in the microwave.

For the best gloss, allow the chocolate to set at room temperature rather than putting it in the refrigerator. You can improve the gloss by stirring in about 1 teaspoon of light cooking oil per 100 g of chocolate after it is melted.

JAMS AND MARMALADES

Sterilising Jars for Bottling and Jam-making

Bottling food and jam-making are marvellous ways to take advantage of gluts in food when they happen. If you want your bottled foods or jams to last from the glut time to the sparse time, it is important to make sure that the bottles or jars are sterile and well sealed when you use them. After putting lots of time and effort into the bottling, it is very disappointing to go to the larder and find that the contents have gone mouldy.

If you have a bottling kit, it should come with instructions on sterilising and sealing. You can still make successful preserves without a bottling kit. Make sure you sterilise the lids as well as the bottles themselves, especially if they have been used before. Choose one of the following ways to sterilise your jars:

• Put them into a preheated oven at 100
–130°C while you prepare the contents.
They will need at least 10 minutes.

• Fill them with water, then stand them in
a large saucepan of boiling water on the
stovetop for 10–15 minutes (or while you
prepare the contents).

• Fill the sink with hot, clean water and
add a teaspoon of household bleach or
sodium metabisulphite (available from
home-brewing shops). Leave the bottles
and lids to soak in this for about an hour.
This method is often best for sterilising
lids which cannot take too much heat.
Immediately before using them, quickly
rinse them out with hot, running water
and drain them, upside down, on a clean
draining rack.

When you have made your jam or
preserve and the jars are ready for use,
take care to keep everything sterile while
you put the mixture in the bottles. All
utensils, like ladles, thermometers and
spoons, should also be sterile. Your hands
must be clean. You can keep a jug of
bleach solution beside the stove to hold
your utensils when you are not using
them. When you need one, run it briefly
under the tap to rinse off the bleach. After
use, rinse off any jam and replace the
utensil in the sterilising solution.

To maintain sterility during bottling:

• Fill the jars to the top with the prepared
food and close them while they are still
hot, for a vacuum seal. Before putting on
the lid, wipe the rim with a clean, moist
cloth (you can soak this in your sterilising
solution if you wish) to remove any spills
then screw the lid on tightly.

• Give added protection to your jams by
melting some candle wax and pouring a
layer of this on top before putting on the
lid. This seals out any air which might be
trapped under the lid and prevents the

growth of mould.

• Added protection for other types of
preserve can be obtained by sitting the
filled and sealed jars in a large saucepan
and filling the saucepan with water to
below the level of the lids. Bring it to the
boil and simmer for 10–15 minutes.

Quicker Jam-making in the Microwave
Do you dream of making the family jams,
jellies and marmalades when the fruit is in
season, but keep putting it off because of
the time involved? If you have a
microwave, you can cut down
considerably on the time and, incidentally,
eliminate the problem of the burnt jam
saucepan. You will still need to spend
some time preparing the fruit but
generally the cooking time will be much
shorter than on the stove top, and you
won't need to do all the stirring.

• Sterilise the jars in the usual way (see
Sterilising Jars for Bottling and Jam-making).
Choose a very large bowl for cooking the
jam — much larger than you think you
need — to allow for the boiling liquid to
climb up the sides.

• Meanwhile, prepare the fruit in the
usual way for your favourite jam or relish
recipe. If you are making marmalade, it
will be more tender if you soak the peel in
water overnight before cooking it. If you
are making a jelly, microwave the fruit in a
covered dish for 20 minutes on High,
stirring halfway through the time. Then
strain out the solids and proceed.

• Use pectin to ensure a good set as there
is much less evaporation with microwaved
jam than with conventionally-cooked jam.
(You can use lemon pips in a cloth bag or
buy pectin powder.)

• Put the fruit (or strained fruit juice) and
pectin into the bowl. Microwave it on
High until it boils — usually about 8 –10
minutes.

• Add the sugar and stir it in well.

(Adding it too early can make the fruit tough, especially in marmalade.) Microwave it on High until it comes back to the boil and allow one minute of full boiling.

• Skim the jam and stir it for a few minutes before pouring it into jars. Seal them in the usual way.

Marmalade Too Tough?

Home-made marmalade is usually much tangier and tastier than the type you buy, but sometimes you may be disappointed with the texture. If your marmalade has rather tough peel, it may be for one of these reasons:

• The peel was not cut finely enough. If it is in big lumps it will take a very long time to soften. Try shredding it more finely or even processing it in the food processor once the pith has been removed.

• The peel was not soaked before cooking. Soaking the peel allows it to start softening before you cook it and it will soften much more quickly in the cooking pan. Next time, try soaking the peel in cold water overnight.

• The marmalade was not cooked long enough before the sugar was added. It needs to be quite soft when the sugar goes in, because the sugar will tend to prevent further softening.

• The marmalade was boiled too fast. Like most foods, the peel tends to toughen if it is boiled very rapidly. Try simmering it rather than having it on full boil next time.

Clearer Marmalade

If your marmalade tends to be cloudy rather than sparkling and clear, this is usually because pith has been included with the orange or grapefruit peel. (Lemon peel doesn't cloud the marmalade as much and it also increases the pectin.) By removing all traces of pith from the peel before using it, your marmalade will be much clearer.

NUTS

Shell Nuts Easily with a Microwave

If you want to make sure your nuts will shell, put them in a microwave dish and add ½ cup (250 ml) of water per 1 cup (125 g) of nuts. Microwave them for 4–5 minutes on High and then drain. The shells should come off easily.

Browning Hazelnuts

Hazelnuts brown best in the oven in their skins. Remove the shells and put them on a tray without removing the skins from around the nut kernels. Cook them for 5–10 minutes in a moderate oven at about 175°C. This will brown the nut and make the skins brittle and dry. When the nuts are cool enough to handle, rub the skins off with a plastic kitchen scourer or a rough cloth.

Stale Nuts

Stale roasted nuts can be revived by heating them at about 180°C for a few minutes. Alternatively, toss roasted or raw nuts in a little hot oil in a frying pan for a few minutes until they look toasted.

Browning Almonds

Almonds are juicier if they are blanched before use. If you want to brown them, remove their skins and bake them on an oven tray at about 175°C for 5–10 minutes. You will have crisp, brown nuts suitable for eating as they are or for cooking.

Alternatively, toss shredded or chopped almonds in a hot pan with half a tablespoon each of butter and cooking oil for a few minutes. This method gives a toasted but juicy nut with a fine buttery coating, suitable for cooking.

Quick Chopped Nuts

Chopped nuts can be used in all sorts of sweet or savoury dishes, as an ingredient in their own right or as a garnish. Chopping by hand is no fun but you can chop nuts quickly and efficiently in a food processor or blender.

Use the slowest speed, if you have more than one to choose from, and process them in very short bursts until they are chopped to the fineness you want. Blending them for longer will give you ground nuts - also very useful if that is what you set out to make!

Keep a jar of chopped nuts handy in the refrigerator (to stop them going rancid). They are good for cake toppings, for adding interest to meat dishes and stuffings, for mixing into sandwich fillings and for various other things.

SAVOURY THINGS

STEAK AND KIDNEY PUDDING

A traditional winter warmer is the steak and kidney pudding, cooked all day until, at night, it is a wonderful golden brown and melts in the mouth.

Add a delicious touch to your steak and kidney puddings by adding a few oysters to the filling. By the end of the cooking, they are no longer identifiably fishy-tasting and have contributed a rich flavour to the pudding. If fresh oysters are not readily available, a tablespoon or two of canned mixed seafood sauce can have a similar effect.

The curry pan
Curries should be thickened not with flour, but by reducing the cooking liquid until it thickens itself. You will need a fairly wide, shallow pan for cooking a curry, to offer a greater surface for evaporation. This should not cause burning, as slow cooking is essential to bring out the flavours of the spices and to make sure any meat is really tender.

Bring out the taste - cook it in advance
Curries are among the few dishes which actually benefit from being made ahead of time and reheated. By making a curry the day before and then reheating it, the flavours of the spices mature and mingle. When a curry is served as soon as it is cooked, the hot elements in the spices, like chilli and ginger, tend to dominate and the taste is not as full as it is when left to develop overnight.

If you are preparing curry for a special occasion, making it ahead of time will free you to spend the time before the meal preparing the accompaniments, rather than cooking the main dish itself.

Home-made curry paste
If you like the richness of home-made blends of spices rather than bought curry powder but you don't always have the time to prepare your own, you can make up a jar of curry paste to store in the refrigerator. Buy bulk individual spices when you have time to go to a specialist foodstore. Toast them, one at a time, in a small frying pan and transfer them to the food processor. Add some fresh root ginger, garlic, lemon grass and ¼–⅓ cup (100 ml) cooking oil (olive is good). Blend them on full speed for a few minutes until they make a smooth paste. If necessary, add some extra oil to moisten the mixture. Scoop out the paste and seal it in a glass screwtop jar. This will store in the

refrigerator for months if necessary. When you want to make a curry, simply spoon out the required amount of paste and sauté it along with the onions before adding the remaining ingredients.

Cooking Papadums

These delicious, crisp lentil slices are ideal to serve with curry and are simple to cook, but they must be light and dry to be really good.

The secret of perfect papadums lies in having the oil really hot but not so hot as to fill the house with the fumes of burning fat. Heat the oil slowly so that it is equally hot on the sides and the middle of the pan. To test when it is ready, drop in a small corner of a papadum. When it starts to sizzle and rises to the surface of the fat, the oil is ready for cooking.

Before you start to cook, prepare a board for draining the finished papadums by covering it with 2–3 layers of paper towel.

Papadums should be cooked one at a time, very quickly (they take less than a minute when the fat is at the right temperature). Drop in a papadum and immediately grasp a fork in each hand. The papadum will sizzle and distort into an odd shape. With the forks, carefully and quickly press down the lifting edges, forcing it flat. Then, quickly turn it over and repeat the action on the other side, to make sure that the whole surface of the papadum has been cooked. Lift it out as soon as it stops expanding, and place it on the paper towel to drain while you cook the next one. It will usually take only a few seconds each side.

For a low-fat diet, some papadums can be cooked in the microwave these days without any fat at all. Make sure they are not left to sit for long before eating as they tend to absorb moisture from the air and go soft. You can revive them, if necessary, in a hot oven for a few minutes before serving.

DUMPLINGS FOR THE STEW

Another favourite winter warmer is stew. You can dress up any stew, and add body to feed extra hungry people, by adding dumplings to the top. The dumplings are simply made by mixing 2 parts (by weight) white or wholemeal self-raising flour with 1 part prepared suet. If you prefer, you can use margarine, rubbed in as though making pastry. Then add just enough cold water to make a soft dough. An average stew would need about 250 g flour to 125 g suet to ¾ cup (180 ml) cold water.

Make sure the stew pan is big enough to give the dumplings plenty of room to rise, as they will certainly do so while they cook.

Mix the dumplings quickly and drop spoonfuls onto the top of the cooked or nearly-cooked stew. Simmer the pot with the lid on for another 20–30 minutes or until the dumplings no longer show specks of fat when opened gently with a fork. The dumplings will absorb the flavours of the gravy and add a warming and filling touch to the dish.

EASY CRUMB COATING FOR FRYING

The worst part of fried crumbed food is the fiddle of coating the pieces. There is an easier way:

• Prepare your seasoned flour and crumbs as usual, but instead of dishes, put each in a plastic bag big enough to hold individual pieces of food. The beaten egg still needs to go in a dish.

• Drop the pieces of food, one at a time into the flour bag, shaking them well. They should each emerge with a good coating of flour.

• Dip the pieces of food into the egg as usual if you are going to coat them with crumbs. For some purposes, a flour coating might be sufficient.

• Now drop them one at a time into the bag of crumbs and shake them. Do this a little more carefully than you did the flour coating, so as not to jostle off the coating you are trying to put on! You should now have coated pieces of food ready to fry, with much less mess than the traditional way. Any leftover flour and crumbs can be tipped into the leftover beaten egg, with a little grated cheese or other flavouring added, and mixed well. It will make a tasty fritter to go with the meal.

RECYCLING FRYING OIL AND DRIPPING

As a rule, oil used for deep-frying will not absorb the flavours of the food it has cooked. After straining the oil through a sieve lined with clean cloth or a paper coffee filter it can be recycled for other cooking.

There is a significant exception to this. If you have fried something with a large amount of hot chilli, the oil can retain the hot part of the chilli flavour and transmit this to the next dish. Oil which has been used for a chilli dish is therefore best re-used only for another hot dish.

To recycle dripping for cooking, pour a little water into the fat after it has cooled but before it solidifies. This will trap the food residues in the bottom of the dish and later the clean fat can be lifted off.this layer.

FRIED RICE FROM LEFTOVERS

Leftover cooked chicken, pork, lamb or beef can be made into a delicious fried rice dish in just a few minutes.

• Cut the meat into bite-sized pieces and toss it in a wok with a little hot oil, some soy sauce, ginger and oyster sauce or your favourite Asian ingredients. (A wok is best for this, but a large frying pan will do. Non-stick is best.)

• Sauté it until it becomes quite toasty-brown on the outside and has soaked up all the sauces in the pan.

• Add some cut up vegetables such as spring onion, capsicum, baby corn, celery and mushrooms, and toss the mixture until the vegetables start to soften. Add some cooked rice and toss the whole lot in the pan vigorously until everything is hot through.

KEEP SALT FREE OF LUMPS

Lumps form in salt because of moisture accumulating in it and then drying out, leaving caked salt. There are several ways to prevent lumps.

You can store salt in an open 'salt-pig' made of porous clay. This absorbs moisture from the salt. In very wet weather, if the salt in the 'pig' becomes moist, put the whole thing in a warm oven for a while to dry out.

Alternatively, you can put a little rice in your salt container. This is handy for table salt, as the rice doesn't shake out of the hole but will absorb the moisture from the salt. Again, if it becomes clogged in damp weather, put it in the oven on a low heat. If you can't heat your salt cellar without damage, empty it into a baking dish first and dry the cellar out separately. Then replace the salt and rice.

Keeping your bulk salt supply in a well-sealed container in the refrigerator will help stop lumps forming.

VINEGAR

If you are on a tight budget, here is a tip for making vinegar go twice as far. Simply divide it in half when you buy it — the old bottle is a good place to put the second half — and top up both bottles with water which has been boiled. After a week it will come up to full strength again.

STONING OLIVES

In Europe it is possible to buy just about any kind of olive in any condition you might need. In other places you may not be able to buy them without stones.

To stone an olive, you will need a small, sharp knife with a narrow, pointed blade.

To stone a green olive, cut across the top, just enough to make a slit into which you can slip the point of the knife. Work the knife point in a spiral next to the stone, until you reach the bottom. Cut the stone free and gently push the olive back into shape again.

Stoning a black olive is easier. These are softer and you can usually slit them lengthwise and ease out the stone with the point of the knife.

PASTA

Does your pasta stick together when you cook it? It needn't if you follow a few simple rules:
• Make sure the pot you cook it in is really big — with space to fit in all the raw pasta and plenty of room for it to move around freely. Have lots of water in the pan and make sure it is boiling rapidly before adding the pasta.
• Sometimes a tablespoon of oil added to the cooking water can help to prevent the pasta sticking.

Ravioli which Stays Whole in the Pot

Ravioli and other filled pastas such as tortellini are more and more popular in today's cuisine. Cooked too vigorously, they are inclined to open and spill their contents into the water, leaving you with unfilled pasta pockets in a soupy, watery liquid.

To avoid losing the contents of your filled pasta, always put it into boiling water, allow it a few moments to return to the boil, then cover the pot with a lid, turn the heat down to a simmer and cook it as long as required. The pasta will cook and stay whole. When you take off the lid, give the pot a good stir and boil it again on High for about a minute before draining it.

For a really delicious taste to your usual tomato topping, stir in up to a tablespoon of pesto (an Italian basil sauce) as it cooks. This will enrich the flavour marvellously.

REVIVE DAMP SNACKS

Savoury snacks certainly aren't appetising when they have gone soft. This is a result of moisture in the food. The snacks can be restored to the peak of their crispness simply by heating:

• In the conventional oven, bake them on 200°C for a few minutes, then cool them on a rack.

• If you have a microwave oven, put them on a dish over a layer or two of paper towel. Microwave them, uncovered, on High for a few seconds. Let them stand for a few minutes to crisp. If they are still soft, repeat the treatment.

DRINKS

TEA BLENDS FOR TASTE

These days tea bags have mostly taken over from leaf tea made in a pot. However, there are still those occasions when it is nicer to serve a steaming pot — when visitors are gathered or when a lot of family members are at home together.

You can make your tea more tasty and distinctive by blending it and storing it in a tea caddy. A packet of ordinary Indian tea can be enhanced by adding ½ cup (45 g) each of 2 or 3 Chinese teas. Try blending in ½ cup (45 g) Jasmine and ½ cup (45 g) of Oolong. Or try ½ cup (45 g) of China Black with 2 tablespoons of well-dried, shredded orange peel. (Dry the peel in the oven or the microwave.) The additions provide a subtle, refreshing touch of flavour which makes a change from the everyday family brew.

GROUND COFFEE THAT KEEPS ITS FLAVOUR

There's nothing quite like the smell of freshly ground coffee but it so rapidly loses its aroma and flavour once the pack is opened. In the freezer, it will keep almost indefinitely in a sealed container or bag and, because it has a low moisture content, it will not stick together in a mass. This means that you can open the pack straight from the freezer, take out enough for a pot of coffee, then return the unused portion.

WEIGHTS & MEASURES

METRIC	IMPERIAL	BRITISH STANDARDS	US STANDARDS
5 ml	0.2 fl oz	1 Aust/NZ teaspoon	
15 ml	0.5 fl oz	1 UK tablespoon	
20 ml	0.6 fl oz	1Aust/NZtablespoon	
28 ml	1 UK fl oz		
30 ml	1 US fl oz		
160 ml	5 fl oz	¼ UK pint / 1 gill	
250 ml	8 fl oz		1 US/Aust cup
300 ml	10 fl oz	1 UK cup	
450 ml	16 fl oz		1 US pint
570 ml	20 fl oz	1 UK pint	
1 litre	35 fl oz		4 Aust cups
2 pints	1 quart		
8 pints	4 quarts		1 gallon

LIQUID MEASURES

Where measures do not have an exact equivalent, they have been rounded to the nearest convenient one for simplicity. As a rule, American measures are slightly smaller than British ones. If in doubt, it doesn't really matter which you use as long as you are consistent. Watch your cooking times, however, if you are using different measures from those of the recipe. You may need to adjust them.

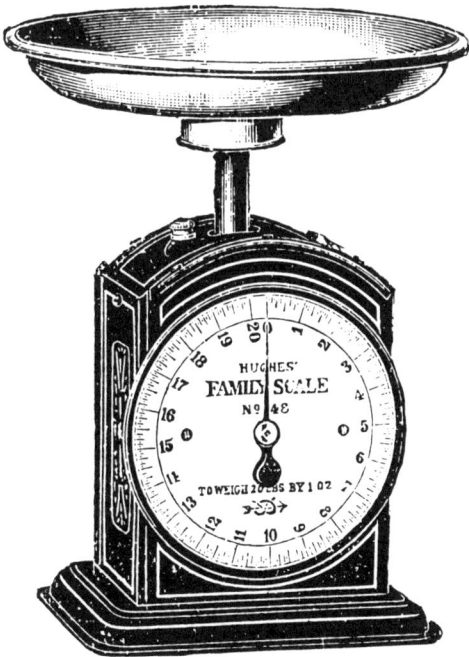

WEIGHTS AND QUANTITIES

This chart, similarly, gives approximations rather than exact amounts. It is based on the Australian Metric Conversion Chart

METRIC WEIGHTS	IMPERIAL WEIGHTS
15 g	½ oz
30 g	1 oz
60 g	2 oz
90 g	3 oz
125 g	4 oz (¼ lb)
155 g	5 oz
185 g	6 oz
220 g	7 oz
250 g	8 oz (½ lb)
280 g	9 oz
315 g	10 oz
345 g	11 oz
375 g	12 oz (¾ lb)
410 g	13 oz
440 g	14 oz
470 g	15 oz
500 g	16 oz (1 lb)
1 kg	32 oz (2 lb)

TEMPERATURE CONVERSION CHARTS

In this chart the temperatures have been rounded to the nearest five degrees for convenience in the kitchen.

FAHRENHEIT	CELSIUS	GAS MARK	WORDING
150	65		
175	80		
200	95		
225	110	Regulo ¼	very slow
250	120	Regulo ½	
275	135	Regulo 1	slow
300	150	Regulo 2	
325	165	Regulo 3	moderately slow
350	180	Regulo 4	moderate/medium
375	190	Regulo 5	moderately hot
400	200	Regulo 6	hot
425	220	Regulo 7	
450	230	Regulo 8	very hot
475	245	Regulo 9	

KITCHEN GLOSSARY

Are there recipes in your books you would like to try if you could understand the instructions? Many cooking terms come from French and, if you haven't met them before, may be unintelligible to a non-French speaker. Other terms are sometimes used in a rather cavalier way as though everyone knows what they mean. If you don't you are at a distinct disadvantage. Here are some terms which might help you to decipher recipes you haven't been able to use.

A la (Au): 'In the manner of' — often refers to a place where the dish originated, *à la paysanne* (country style) or *à la normande* (Normandy style). It can mean 'with' as in *Steak au Poivre*, or Pepper Steak.

Aspic: A savoury jelly (generally made from bones of meat or fish) used for setting or decorating cold foods.

Au gratin: A dish with a creamy sauce, sprinkled with butter and breadcrumbs and/or cheese and baked or grilled to brown and crisp the top.

Bain marie: A wide dish (can be a baking dish or larger saucepan) which is half filled with water and used to hold another dish or saucepan containing the food, eg a custard or an egg dish. The water is kept at or near boiling so the food in the inner pan simmers but does not boil or burn. (This is the same idea as in a double boiler.)

Baking blind: This refers to cooking a pastry shell on its own before adding the filling. It is used to prevent the bottom of the pastry from going soggy during cooking with the filling. To prevent the sides of the shell from collapsing, a layer of foil is pressed into it or it is lined with greaseproof paper and filled with beans or rice. The whole thing is then baked until the pastry is set but not completely cooked. The liner is removed and the beans (if used) returned to their jar for re-use. The pastry is returned to the oven to finish cooking and dry before the filling is added.

Baking: To cook in the oven using dry heat. This is mostly used for cakes, breads, pies and biscuits. (Meats cooked this way are called *roast*).

Barding: This is a technique of covering all or part of a roast, like a whole baked fillet of beef or the breast of poultry, with strips of fat or bacon before cooking to prevent it drying.

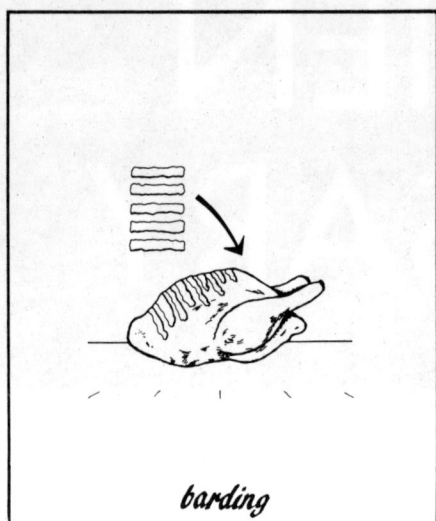

barding

Basting: Moistening and flavouring meat or fish during cooking by pouring or spooning liquid (often its own juices from the bottom of the pan) over it.

Batter: A runny mixture, usually made from flour, eggs and water or milk, which is beaten. It is generally used for coating foods before frying but can also be baked as a sweet or savoury pudding.

Beating: Vigorously mixing or turning a food with a spoon, fork or mixer in such a way as to trap air in it and make it a smooth, evenly-blended texture.

Bechamel: A type of creamy French white sauce.

Beurre manié: A smooth mixture of flour and butter, in equal quantities, stirred into soups or stews as a thickening agent.

Binding: Combining ingredients to make a stable mixture, eg adding eggs or cream to a soup or sauce to thicken it or to dry ingredients to hold them together.

Bisque: A creamy type of soup, usually based on seafood.

Blanching: Immersing food briefly into boiling water in order to whiten it, to loosen the skin, to remove excess salt or flavour (eg from bacon) or to kill surface organisms before preserving the food in some way.

Blanquette: Meat stew to which milk, cream or egg yolk is added to give a creamy pale finish.

Blending: Mixing ingredients smoothly and evenly together.

Boiling: Heating liquid to 100°C (212°F) and maintaining it there. This is the point where bubbles continuously form and break at the surface.

Boning: Removing the bones from meat or fish.

Bouillon: Clear soup, broth or stock made with meat, fish or vegetables.

Bouquet garni: A mixture of herbs tied together, used to flavour savoury dishes and removed after cooking. Traditionally it consists of parsley, thyme, bay and pepper but it can be made up of whatever herbs are suitable to the dish.

Braising: Browning meat or fish (or blanching vegetables) and then cooking them slowly in a tightly-lidded pan with a little liquid to keep the food moist.

Breading: (Also called **Crumbing**) Rolling food in a coating of breadcrumbs before cooking.

Broiling: Cooking food by direct heat above or below, eg by electric, gas or charcoal grilling (same as **grilling**).

Browning: This can either mean frying meat quickly to seal the outside before stewing it or putting a cooked dish under a grill or in a hot oven for a time to make the surface brown.

Caramelising: Melting sugar, sometimes

with other ingredients, slowly in a thick bottomed pan, stirring continuously, until it turns syrupy and golden brown.

Casserole: A stew cooked slowly in the oven in a dish with a well-fitting lid. It is usually served in the same dish.

Chaudfroid: A jellied, creamy sauce used to dress cold fish or meat. (For game it is usually made a rich brown colour.)

Chilling: Cooling in the refrigerator until cold.

Chopping: Cutting into very small pieces with a quick action, using a sharp knife or chopper. Traditionally, the tip of the blade is held down while the handle is bounced quickly up and down, moving across the food.

Chowder: A seafood soup, often substantial enough to be a meal on its own.

Clarifying: Removing impurities from a liquid or fat. It can refer to removing food particles from clear stocks, soups or broths by straining (sometimes with crushed eggshells added to make the liquid clearer) or to removing water and/or sediment from fat, eg butter.

Coating: Covering food with another ingredient. It can refer to rolling food in flour or breadcrumbs before cooking or to dressing food with a sauce before serving. A **coating consistency** in a batter or mixture is like thinnish cream. It is thick enough to coat the back of a spoon so you can see the shape but the colour is obscured.

Cocotte: A covered, heatproof dish (normally pottery or cast iron), often small for individual servings.

Coddling: Boiling eggs softly by putting them into boiling water and then removing them from the heat so they can

cook slowly as they stand in the water.

Compote: Stewed fruit served hot or cold.

Consistency: Texture.

Cooling: Allowing food to stand at room temperature (not in the refrigerator) until it no longer feels warm.

Court bouillon: Another name for the liquid (stock or broth), generally made from meat, fish or vegetables, in which savoury food is cooked for added flavour.

Creaming: Mixing or working one or more ingredients to make a smooth, light paste. It most often refers to mixing butter and sugar together in cake making.

Crimping: Pressing a fluted decoration into the edge of a pie, tart or biscuit before cooking.

Croquettes: A flattened ball or sausage shaped patty of meat, fish or vegetables, coated with breadcrumbs and fried (similar to **rissoles**).

Croute: This can refer to a piece of toast or fried bread on which some entrees are served, or to a pastry crust cooked on the outside of a pâté or cut of meat.

Croutons: Small, crisp cubes of fried, toasted or oven dried bread used in soups and some salads.

Crumbing: (Also called **Breading**) Rolling food in a coating of breadcrumbs before cooking.

Curd: The solid portion of milk when it has been soured with acid (lemon or vinegar) or with rennet (junket) or a similar textured food made from soy beans. This name is also sometimes given to thick spreads made from fruit cooked with egg yolks, butter and sugar, eg lemon curd.

Cutting-in: A method of combining fat and flour in pastry making by cutting quickly through the fat again and again with one or two knives or with a food processor, until the ingredients are combined. It keeps the food cooler than rubbing in the fat with a warm hand.

Dariole: A traditional small, shaped mould for jellies and puddings.

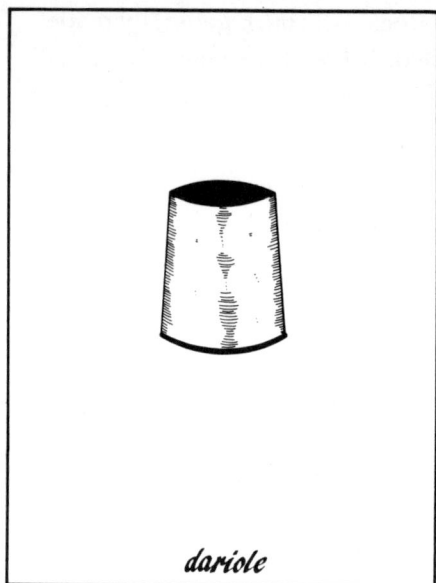

dariole

Deep-frying: Cooking in hot fat which totally immerses the food until it is crisp and golden. (Also called **French-frying**).

Devilling: Grilling or frying food with hot, spicy seasonings.

Dicing: Cutting food into small cubes, usually about 1cm.

Disjointing: (Sometimes called **jointing**) cutting meat, usually poultry, apart into portions by dividing at the joints.

Dough: A thick, raw mixture of flour and liquid to be made into bread, scones or biscuits.

Dredging: Dusting a fine layer of a dry ingredient like sugar or flour in a coating over the surface of a food. This can be done by sprinkling from the fingers, shaking a fine sieve over the food or using a special sifter or dredger.

Dripping: Rendered down fat, from cooking meat or just from pieces of raw fat melted down.

Dropping (. . . **Consistency**): The texture of a raw cake or pudding mixture which is like a very thick cream. Fill a spoon with the mixture and hold it on its side. The mixture should gently slide off the spoon without jerking it.

Duxelles: A dry mixture of finely-chopped vegetables, usually onion and mushrooms, sautéed (fried) in butter and used to flavour meat or fish dishes during cooking.

Entree: A small hot or cold savoury dish served before a main course as an appetiser. In America this term may refer to the main course.

Escalope: A thin, lean slice of meat, usually veal. It is usually fried quickly in breadcrumbs or with a savoury sauce.

Farce/forcemeat: A stuffing for meat, fish or vegetables. It is usually made from a mixture of meat (often ham or bacon) or fish (especially shellfish) and/or breadcrumbs with herbs and seasonings. It may also contain chopped dried fruits, nuts or other strongly-flavoured foods.

Fillet: This can refer to a cut of meat or fish which contains no bones. It is usually cut off the bone lengthways, making it very tender. It can also refer to the act of cutting off the fillet — filleting.

Fines herbes: This is a mixture of finely chopped dried herbs, often used in egg dishes.

Fish fumet: A highly concentrated fish stock used for poaching fish dishes.

Flaking: Breaking food (especially fish) into small pieces with a fork. It is generally used as a method for deciding whether it is cooked.

Flaming (flambé): Pouring alcohol over a dish and igniting it. It is used to add a subtle burnt sugar taste as well as for display while serving.

Folding in: An action of gently combining dry and wet ingredients by hand, especially when the wet ingredients (eg egg white or cream) have been whisked to trap air first. By repeatedly turning the mixture over gently with a spatula, (often adding the dry ingredients gradually) the dry ingredients can be added without losing the lightness. Lightness of touch is essential to avoid breaking the air bubbles in the mixture.

Fool: Dessert made by folding fruit purée through whipped cream.

Fricassee: A dish consisting of white meat braised in a light, creamy sauce.

Fritter: Meat, fish, vegetables or fruit dipped into batter and deep fried.

Frosting: A type of soft American icing, or a method of decorating the edges of glasses by dipping them into egg white and then caster sugar (often coloured with food dye).

Frying: Cooking food in hot fat or oil over a direct heat source.

Fumet: A highly concentrated fish or meat stock.

Galantine: A cold dish of rolled and pressed cooked meat (sometimes with ingredients of contrasting colour rolled into the centre, eg darker meats, olives or capsicums), often decorated with a glaze or with breadcrumbs on the surface.

Garnish: An edible decoration for a dish, usually chosen also to enhance the flavour. It may be fruit or vegetable, such as ornamentally-cut salad vegetables, parsley, strawberries or seed sprouts; it may be a bakery food, such as croutons or pastry shapes or it may be small pieces of meat or shellfish. Garnish is limited only by your imagination.

Glaze: A thin, glossy coating to decorate sweet or savoury food. Moist glazes may be syrup or aspic, highly concentrated homemade meat or fish stock, or fruit juices thickened with cornflour or arrowroot. Dry glazes can be given to baked foods like pastry or cakes by brushing with milk or egg before baking.

Grating: Cutting food into shreds with a grater (by hand or with a food processor). This is more successful with firm foods and some need to be chilled before they will grate well.

Greasing: Preparing a dish for baking by rubbing fat or oil well into the surface. This prevents food sticking.

Grilling: Cooking food by direct heat under or over a hot gas flame, charcoal or electric element (same as **Broiling**).

Grinding: Crushing hard foods like coffee beans, peppercorns or nuts to a fine or coarse powder by means of a special mill. In American recipes this term also applies to the mincing of meat.

Homogenised: Liquid containing fat (eg milk) which has been 'emulsified' — that is mixed together in such a way that the fat will not separate out into a separate layer again.

Hors d'oeuvre: A small (usually cold) appetiser served as a starter to a meal.

Infusing: Steeping food in hot liquid (usually water) for a while until the flavours of the food are taken up by the liquid (an infusion).

Jardinière: Mixed fresh vegetables, cut or diced, served as a garnish to a savoury dish.

Julienne: Finely cut strips of crisp vegetables, especially carrots and celery, about the size of matches, used as a garnish.

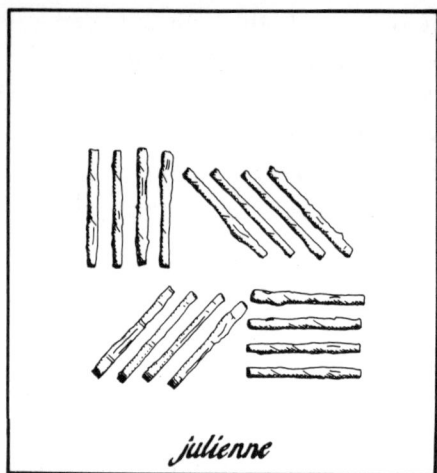

julienne

Kneading: Rhythmically folding and pressing dough (especially yeast dough) to mix it thoroughly and to break down the gluten in the flour. Pastry is usually kneaded lightly and briefly, while bread dough should be kneaded vigorously for at least 10 minutes.

Knocking back: Punching or pressing down a risen yeast dough to expel the air, before kneading it again and shaping it.

Lard: Rendered down pork fat. This has a smooth consistency and is used to give shortness to pastry. **Larding** is also the name of a process of threading strips of fatty bacon or pork fat into meat for roasting to prevent it drying out. These strips are called **lardons** (see also *Barding* above).

Liaison: Thickening sauces or soups by adding flour, cornflour, potato or pea flour, *beurre manié*, egg yolk or cream.

Lukewarm: A temperature which is about the same as blood heat — it should feel just warm to the hand, about 38°C (100°F).

Macedoine: Diced mixed fruit or vegetables as a garnish or as a salad.

Macerating: Soaking fruit in liqueur or syrup.

Marinade: A mixture of liquids (eg wine, lemon juice, oil, piquant sauces or, in the case of fruit, liqueur or syrup) and seasonings (herbs and spices) in which food is left to soak for a period of time before cooking. It adds flavour and, for meats, also serves to tenderise the food.

Marinating: The process of steeping a food in a marinade.

Masking: This refers both to the process of coating a cooked dish with a glaze, jelly or sauce (in which it may be chilled if a cold dish) and to the process of lining a mould with a thin layer of jelly for decoration before the main contents of the mould are added.

Mincing: Chopping or processing food with a knife or machine to reduce it to very small particles.

Mirepoix: A mixture of diced vegetables (usually carrots, celery and onion), sometimes with ham or bacon pieces, sauteed in butter and used in cooking meat or fish dishes.

Mousse: A smooth, creamy dish, made by folding together eggs, cream and a flavouring like fruit puree or chocolate with sugar (for a dessert mousse), or seafood or chicken (for a savoury mousse). Gelatine is often used to set mousse, especially savoury ones.

Noisettes: Small, thick rounds of trimmed red meat, often lamb.

Oven frying: Cooking food in hot oil in an uncovered dish in the oven.

Panada: A thick sauce used to bind mixtures of ingredients to make croquettes.

Papillote: *En papillote* refers to cooking food wrapped in a parcel of foil or paper.

Parboiling: Partly cooking food by boiling, before finishing the cooking by some other method. It is commonly used to soften foods quickly when they are then to be roasted or fried.

Paring: Peeling or trimming, especially vegetables or fruits with skins.

Pasteurised: A process of killing bacteria in food or milk by raising the temperature just below boiling point.

Petits fours: These are very small, decorated cakes, usually very rich, served at the end of a meal with coffee.

Piping: A technique for squeezing cream, icing, meringue or dough out of a bag with a shaped nozzle to decorate a sweet dish or make a biscuit or pastry of a particular shape. It can also be used for potatoes in savoury dishes.

Pitting: Removing the seeds or stones from fruit such as cherries.

Poaching: Cooking meat, fish, eggs, vegetables or fruits covered in gently simmering liquid.

Pot roast: A method of cooking less tender joints of meat in a saucepan with some fat and a little liquid.

Pulses: The name given to peas, beans and lentils. In cooking, this most often refers to them in their dried form.

Purée: A fine, smooth, pulverised paste of any food or mixture of foods (usually cooked) with the consistency of cream thick or thin. It can be fruit (eg apple), vegetable eg pumpkin, meat or fish.

Ragout: A type of stew.

Ramekin: A small pottery dish for cooking and serving individual portions of a recipe.

Réchauffé: A word for reheated food.

Reducing: Cooking a liquid over a high heat with no lid, so that much of the water evaporates, leaving a more concentrated liquid or thick sauce.

Render: To melt fat, by itself or from meat, by slow cooking.

Rennet: An enzyme which curdles milk to make cheese or junket.

Rissoles: Small patties of meat or fish mixtures which are usually crumbed and then fried (similar to **croquettes**).

Roast: Cook meat in an oven in an open pan or on a spit.

Roux: A mixture of equal quantities of flour and fat (butter or margarine), cooked together in a saucepan to make a base for a sauce. When the roux starts to sizzle, it is removed from the heat and milk, stock or water are added slowly, stirred continuously and returned to the heat from time to time, until the sauce has reached the desired consistency.

Rubbing in: A method of combining fat and flour in pastry making or for making biscuits or some cakes. It gives a short texture to the finished food.

Salmi: A stew style dish of roast meat, especially game, which is cooked again in a rich wine sauce after roasting.

Sauté: A method of cooking or part-cooking food by shaking and tossing it quickly in a little hot oil or butter.

Scalding: Heating food (especially milk

or cream) to just below boiling point to prevent it burning. Alternatively it can refer to pouring boiling water quickly over a food to remove feathers or hair (from meat) or skins (from fruit or vegetables).

Scalloping: Decorating the edge of a pie crust by pressing it at regular intervals with a knife to make little curves.

Scoring: Making regular cuts, usually through skin, on meat such as pork or on fish or vegetables, to improve the cooking process.

Searing: Browning and sealing the surface of meat quickly in a hot pan before cooking it more slowly. It keeps the juices in during the slower part of the cooking.

Seasoning: Any mixture of salt, pepper, herbs, spices and other flavourings used to improve savoury dishes.

Shortening: Fat used to give a light, crisp texture to pastry or biscuits. Fat with the least liquid (eg lard) gives the best shortening quality.

Sieving: Forcing food through a sieve, often with the back of a wooden spoon, to make its consistency more smooth and even and to remove large particles.

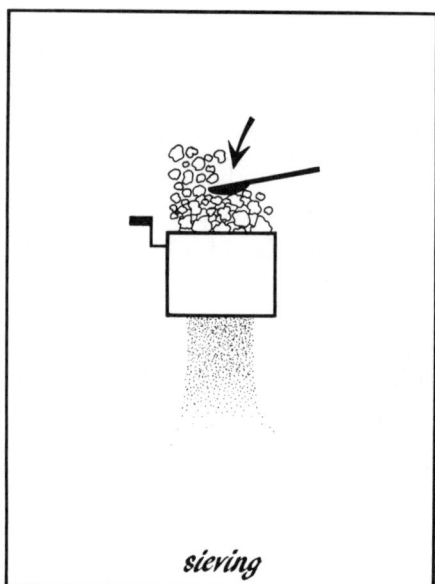

sieving

Sifting: Finely sieving dry food such as flour or icing sugar to remove lumps.

Simmering: Cooking food at a temperature just below boiling to keep it tender. Simmering can be recognised by fine bubbles just rising to the surface as the food cooks. Food which boils actively tends to become tough.

Skimming: Removing fat or scum from the surface of a liquid during or after cooking, using paper towel or a spoon.

Steaming: Cooking food by means of steam. Usually the food is put in a pierced steamer above a pan of boiling water so that the steam can rise through the holes and cook the food.

Steeping: Pouring hot liquid over food and allowing it to stand in it. This is done to soften dried foods or to extract colour or flavour from them.

Stewing: Cooking mixtures of meat, vegetables and/or fish together slowly over a long time so that the textures soften and the flavours mingle together.

Stock: A flavoured liquid used in cooking to enhance the flavour of foods. It is usually made from meat or fish and strongly-flavoured vegetables or vegetable trimmings, seasoned with herbs. These are cooked for a long time and then strained to remove the solids, leaving a well-flavoured liquid (see also *Bouillon*).

Truss: Tie up meat, especially poultry, before cooking.

Whisking: Rapidly beating food such as egg whites or cream with a whisk or in an electric mixer or food processor to incorporate the maximum amount of air. This is also called **whipping**.

Zest/rind: The outer skin of citrus fruit, finely grated. This contains oil which gives a strong citrus flavour.

HERB GLOSSARY

Basil: The best variety for cooking is 'sweet basil'. It has a pungent, slightly liquorice flavour and goes well with dishes rich in tomato, especially soups, pastas, rice dishes and stews. It is also delicious finely chopped and sprinkled on salads.

Chilli: Chilli is a variety of very hot pepper, often sold whole or ground on its own to add to meat or vegetable dishes. It is an important ingredient in curries and Mexican cooking. Commercially-prepared chilli powder generally combines ground chilli with a proportion of cumin and oregano. If you are mixing something to your own taste, commercial chilli powder may be best. If you are blending spices according to a particular recipe, check whether you need 'chilli' or 'chilli powder'.

Cloves: Cloves are very strong and aromatic. In small amounts they blend well with spices like cinnamon or nutmeg. They go well with cakes, cooked apples, oranges, pineapple, pork, ham and pickles but should be used sparingly or they will overpower the dish.

Coriander: This can be used as a herb, either fresh or dried, in its green form, or the seeds can be dried and ground as a spice. The fresh form is quite strong, with a rather sweet, perfumy aroma, and goes well in salads, soups and light cooked dishes. It complements celery especially well. The ground seeds have an almost nutty flavour, and go well with savoury meat dishes. Coriander seed is a common ingredient in curries and blends well into many rich and spicy foods.

Dill: This herb, best used fresh, is good in salads, particularly cucumber salad, and pickles. It also goes well with lightly-cooked vegetables, fish and meat dishes. It can also be sprinkled on bread before baking. In richer dishes, its flavour is likely to be swamped by others. Its seeds are often used in pickles and are also good in vegetable dishes.

Garlic: A member of the onion family, this is not really a herb or a spice but is an important flavouring ingredient. It is usually finely chopped or crushed and sautéed with onion at the beginning of preparation of a dish. It goes well with any meat dish but needs to be used in moderation with fish or vegetables because of its dominating aroma.

Ginger: This most versatile spice has a hot, tangy flavour and can be used, finely chopped, in its fresh form or as a powder. The fresh form has a fuller flavour. It goes with a huge range of sweet and savoury dishes, especially in oriental cooking. Try using it in sauces, with fruit, in mulled wine, with fish and with a variety of meats, as well as in cakes and puddings.

Mustard: Mustard can be eaten in different forms. As a seedling it makes a delicious addition to salads along with another seedling — cress. The more common use, though, is as a seed — ground or whole. The commercial mustard we usually use is actually made from mustard seeds and other ingredients. Mustard need not only be a condiment. It is good in sauces (especially cheese or white sauces), salad dressings and pickles, in a marinade for roast meat, or in the basting juices as you cook your roast. Or use the seeds themselves to add a hot, dusky flavour to savoury dishes. It is also good cooked with some bland vegetables, like cabbage. Start with only a little, though, as it is easy to overdo.

Nutmeg: This rich, sweet-smelling spice goes with almost anything. Along with cinnamon and ginger, it goes into commercial 'mixed spice' blends. It keeps better in the nut form but then requires grating. Use it in savoury dishes, in cakes, on cheesecakes, in milk drinks and almost anything else you can think of.

Oregano: This herb is closely related to marjoram and they can be substituted for each other if necessary. It goes well with Mediterranean and Mexican foods, roast meats, pizzas, marinades and anything containing tomatoes.

Paprika: This richly-coloured and mild flavoured spice is the dried and ground fruit of a red sweet pepper. It is very good used generously in casseroles, soups and cheese dishes or, in small quantities, with chicken, veal or seafood. It is also very good as a decoration, shaken over cheese dishes, white sauces; in fact any savoury dish which looks pale and bland.

Parsley: This herb is best fresh, though it can be used dried. In its fresh form it is rich in vitamin C, carotene and some organic salts needed by the body. It adds flavour to meat dishes and stuffings, casseroles and pies, fish, vegetables, eggs and sauces.

Rosemary: This herb's warm, woody taste goes well with lamb or veal but is also good in casseroles and soups, vegetable dishes and breads or scones. Also, sprinkle it over grilled or barbecued meat.

INDEX

pumpkin, microwave
cooking 74

R

radish garnish 29
ravioli 110
recipe books, protecting 8
refrigerators 10–11
reheating
casseroles and stews 100
frozen foods 100
rice 74
roasts
chicken 63
cooking time 62
larding 62
microwave cooking 63–4
pork 63
potatoes 73–4
roux 94
rubber gloves 7

S

salads 74–5
salt, preventing lumps 109
sandwiches, heating in the
microwave
oven 23
saucepans see pans
sauces
for dessert 94
for fish 58–9
lumpy 93
microwave cooking 21
preventing curdling 93
roux 94
skinless 94
savouries
pastry 31
reviving 110

screwtop lids 8
scuffmarks 6
separating eggs 53–4
shellfish, safe to eat 37–8
shortcrust pastry 86–7
shrimps see prawns
silverware
cleaning 13
storing 13
sinks, blocked 6–7
smells
cabbage 70
cigarette 5
fish 10, 58
onions 72
soufflés, collapsed 89
soup
clarifying 26
meat 95
over-salted 95
removing fat 42
thickening 94
tomato 95
sour milk 54–5
spices, choosing and
storing 72
sponge cakes 83
stainless steel stains 14
stains
on glassware 11
heat stains on
furniture 15
on marble and
alabaster 15
moisture rings on
furniture 14
on stainless steel 14
tea and coffee 14
steak and kidney
pudding 107

steam burns 37
steel wool 7
stews
dumplings 108
reheating 100
thickening 94
stir fry 42
stocks, removing fat from 42
stove
cleaning 10
saucepan placement 36
strawberry afternoon tea 32
strudel 82
stuffings 65
sugar
brown, removing
lumps 101
decoration 30
Swiss rolls, preventing
cracking 82

T

taco shells, heating in the
microwave
oven 23–4
taps, cleaning 6
tasting bowls 38
tea
blending 111
bulk brewing 33
stains 14
temperature conversion 114
tempering glassware 11
tenderising tough meat 66
terrazzo floors, cleaning 6
thawing in the microwave
oven 24–5, 100
thickening 94
toaster, cleaning crumbs 9
tobacco smells 5

toffee 32–3
tomato paste, freezing 101
tomatoes
freezing 71
skinning 75
soup 95

V

vacuum flasks 15
van dyck fish tails 57
vegetables
blanching 71
garnishing with 28–9
microwave cooking 70
storing 97–8
vinegar, stretching 110
vitamins 40–1

W

water
conservation 47
poisons in 47
pollution 47
weevils 98–9
weights 113
whey 55
whipped cream,
extending 54
wholemeal breads 90–1
wooden dishes 15
wooden furniture
stains 14–15
wounds, kitchen hygiene 38

Y

yoghurt, thickening 55

Have all the Answers at your Fingertips with the

Bay Books Ultimate Hints Series

The Ultimate book of GARDENING HINTS
Hundreds of tips to save you time and money in the garden

The Ultimate book of FISHING HINTS
Hundreds of tips to help you catch more fish
STEVE STARLING

The Ultimate book of HOME REPAIRS
DIETER MYLIUS

THE ULTIMATE BOOK OF HOUSEHOLD HINTS
Hundreds of hints and tips (and long-kept secrets!) to save you time and money in the home, the kitchen and the garden
Bay Books

THE ULTIMATE BOOK OF MICROWAVE HINTS
Joan McDermott's invaluable hints and tips to help you make the most of your microwave

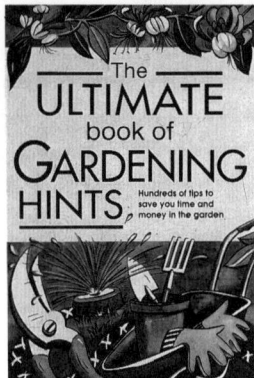

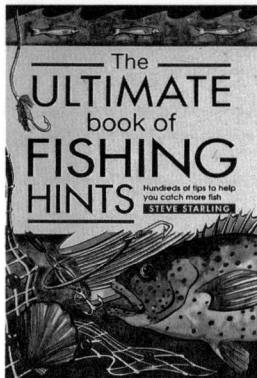

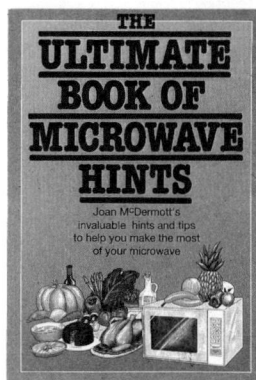

If these titles are not available from your regular stockists, please contact the HarperCollins Sales Office in your State:

WESTERN AUSTRALIA	SOUTH AUSTRALIA	QUEENSLAND	VICTORIA	NEW SOUTH WALES
Suite 2 , 25 Belgravia St	Unit 1 , 1-7 Union St	643 Kessels Road	22-24 Joseph Street	25 Ryde Road
BELMONT WA 6104	STEPNEY SA 5069	UPPER MOUNT GRAVATT	NORTH BLACKBURN	PYMBLE NSW 2073
TEL: (09) 479 4988	TEL: (08) 363 0122	QLD 4122	VIC 3130	TEL: (02) 952 5000
FAX: (09) 478 3248	FAX: (08) 363 1653	TEL: (07) 849 7855	TEL: (03) 895 8100	FAX: (02) 952 5777
		FAX: (07) 349 8286	FAX: (03) 895 8199	